Empowered by Slavery

A History of Political Power and Slavery in Early America

ADAM PLATTS

Platts, Adam

Empowered by Slavery: A History of Political Power and

Slavery in Early America.

Includes bibliography and notes.

ISBN 978-1-329-52841-3

Published in the United States of America.

Contents

Empowered by Slavery

Introduction

Empowered by Slavery examines how the institution of slavery was an integral part of early America's culture and civilization. It describes the power dynamics within antebellum America that permitted the use of African American slave labor to be ruthlessly exploited by America's political, military, and industrial leaders prior to the Civil War. Seven specific slave plantations are examined in this book, along with the plantation owners, as examples of the exploitative system that made a small number of white men extraordinarily wealthy. America's founding generation from the 1700s struggled with the ethical and moral questions surrounding slavery, but many of these wealthy and influential individuals didn't dare disrupt the system that made them so rich. Succeeding generations in the 1800s also grappled with these questions, and they too continued to do so while profiting from slavery being part and parcel of the culture and civilization.

Slavery is the use of force, manipulation, and coercion to entrap men, women, and children and exploit their labor. For the slave it means the loss of one's freedoms, including the freedom of movement, and the loss of legal rights. For the slave owner it means owning human beings and benefitting personally from their labor. In all respects, slavery is an evil institution that has gone on for millennia despite the profoundly savage violation of human rights rooted in its core.

Slavery can be traced back in history to ancient Sumeria, around the year 3500 BCE, but it likely existed long before that too, and coincided with the rise of agricultural civilizations around the world. From Sumeria slavery spread like a terrible disease to other civilizations in the ancient world, and eventually lodged itself in the fabric of Greece and Rome. Slavery existed in Egypt during The New Kingdom of 1558 to 1080 BCE. The Israelites were held captive in Egypt from the time of Seti I in 1318 BCE, to the rule of Ramses II in 1304 BCE. And slavery continued to survive as an institution of Ptolemaic Egypt in 305 BCE. In China slavery existed during the Qin Dynasty as far back as 221 BCE. Muslim merchants and Viking raiders made their own sordid contributions to the dark history of slavery during Europe's Middle Ages.

The enlightenment era, defined by the use of reason to understand the world, and by the value placed on individualism and liberty in Europe during the 1700s, regrettably coincided with a rapid expansion of enslavement in the Americas. The enlightenment that ushered in greater knowledge and power was tangentially responsible for bringing unfathomable darkness to ever greater multitudes. The light of knowledge sparked a massive inferno.

In America, the first seeds of the institution of slavery were planted in the fertile fields of the Chesapeak Bay area by the English in the 1600s. It took hold and spread quickly. Among the first people of African descent to arrive in Virginia were a small number of twenty slaves transported to North America aboard The White Lion, a privateer ship. The privateers had seized the human cargo on board the Sao Jao Bautista, a slave ship from Portugal, and then landed in Jamestown in 1619.

Socio-political changes in the late 1600s then led to vastly larger numbers of slaves being imported to England's North American colonies. When the Royal African Company lost its monopoly on the slave trade it opened the flood gates for many more competing interests to engage in human trafficking. Countless innocent people were captured in Africa, stuffed onto cramped ships, and hastily transported from the west coast of the continent to the Americas, five thousand miles across the Atlantic Ocean. One quarter of all the slaves destined for the Chesapeake died during their first year of captivity.

It must have been a tragically surreal experience

for those who were captured in Africa, forced to march long distances to remote seaports, and then made to endure the miserable conditions within the bowels of a ship as it rocked and lurched for thousands of miles across the open sea. The whole experience, from the point of capture, to the final debarkation from the slave ship, is referred to as "the middle passage," a journey that ended in death for many along the way, and a journey that began an unfortunate life of enslavement for the others.

British dealers were responsible for importing 20,000 slaves annually to the English colony, and by 1740 roughly forty percent of Virginia's population was of African descent, which is to say that forty percent of humanity in the colony of Virginia lived as slaves.

It is estimated that over 600,000 African slaves were brought to plantations in physical locations that are now part of the United States. This total represented just a small fraction of the overall slave population that was imported to the New World. Ninety percent or more were delivered to slave plantations in the Caribbean and South America.

In the late 1700s events on the eastern side of North America transformed the region from being imperially controlled, to independently autonomous. The United States of America was formed because former subjects of the English crown wanted their freedom and self-government. They declared to the world that it was unjust for them to be held captive by a European monarchy, and they fought a war to win their freedom. Among the American rebels to challenge the royal authority of the English crown were wealthy white plantation owners who built their personal fortunes on the backs of enslaved people of African descent.

Prior to the American Revolution and the birth of the United States a 1772 legal case in Britain decided that there was no legal justification for slavery in English law. Four years before its North American colonies declared their independence, England decided to exit the slave business altogether after knowingly and willfully participating in it for 153 years. The plague of slavery in its former colonies, however, would continue on long after.

Over several decades the cash crop businesses of tobacco, sugar, and cotton grew exponentially. The number of slave plantations within the United States could be counted in the thousands. In the states of North and South Carolina alone there were scores of counties with large numbers of plantations in each.

Hundreds of thousands of people were shackled in the chains of human bondage and made to endure unimaginably horrific events during their lives. "Slavery is the next thing to hell," said the famous African American abolitionist Harriet Tubman. And President Abraham Lincoln once said, "Whenever I hear anyone arguing for slavery, I feel a strong impulse to see it tried on him personally." Despite the deep moral and ethical questions associated with slavery, the institution continued to exist within the culture of early America because it was so closely tied to the power enjoyed by a small minority of large plantation owners who accumulated their great wealth by owning hundreds of slaves. And the paramount question of the day in the life of the young democratic nation during the middle of the 1800s was: who would take up arms against the sea of troubles perpetuated by the institution of slavery? "Power concedes nothing without a demand," said the former slave and abolitionist Frederick Douglass. "It never did and it never will."

one

George Washington's Mount Vernon

Empowered by Slavery

Chapter 1: George Washington's Mount Vernon

A relatively small number of Americans of European descent were the principal benefactors of African slavery in the English colonies that would become the United States. Great fortunes were amassed by some slave-owning families who were among the first generations of Euro-Americans. With political savvy, good business sense, and a little bit of luck, they were able to increase and fortify their wealth and power. They reinvested their profits by constantly and consistently acquiring larger tracts of land and a greater number of slaves. The more they invested, the more they realized greater returns. Many of those who depended upon the exploitation of black slave labor for their wealth and status in American society included prominent political, military, and business leaders.

George Washington, America's Revolutionary War hero and first President, was also a slave plantation owner who possessed more than one hundred slaves in his lifetime. The plantation that he called home was Mount Vernon, a wealthy estate overlooking the Potomac.

Washington was born into a family that owned slaves for generations and they became very wealthy from the labor those slaves produced. George Washington's great grandfather, John Washington, left England in 1657 to seek his fortunes in the American colonies. John's descendants owned and operated tobacco plantations, became very wealthy, and married into other plantation owning families. Augustine Washington, the father of George Washington, also married a woman from a tobacco planter family. Eleven months after their marriage, George Washington was born. Washington was a fourth generation American, born into a family whose wealth had been steadily increasing through the decades based on their exploitation of slave labor.

11

Augustine Washington owned the Wakefield tobacco plantation by Bridges Creek in Virginia's Westmoreland County, and it was here that George was born in 1732. Wakefield was just sixty miles north of Jamestown, the original English colony founded in 1607. Though it was George's first home, Wakefield wasn't his home for long because Augustine moved his family to the Little Hunting Creek plantation in 1735, and then again to the Ferry Farm plantation in 1738. Washington's father eventually owned over 10,700 acres, and the productive value of his land was directly related to his ownership of many black slaves. The race-based slave and master system was an accepted norm when Washington was a child. To Washington, white ownership of black slaves was as normal as any other institution in his society, from religion, to trade, to politics. It was part of the culture.

In 1743, before George Washington's teenage years, Augustine passed away, and the bulk of his estate went to the eldest son Lawrence, including the Little Hunting Creek Plantation - later renamed Mount Vernon. Augustine's other son from his first marriage inherited the Wakefield plantation, while George, as the eldest son from the second marriage, received the Ferry Farm plantation. Perhaps sensing a strained relationship between the fourteen year old George Washington and his mother, Lawrence invited George to come live with him at Mount Vernon. Then Washington's fortunes seemed to improve again when Lawrence married into one of the wealthiest families in all the colonies. But tragedy struck when three of Lawrence's children died, and he himself came down with tuberculosis.

In an effort to improve his health, Lawrence fled to Barbados, accompanied by George, and then to Bermuda. But his health didn't improve, and Lawrence died after returning to Mount Vernon. Lawrence's wife Anne held the estate in trust for their only surviving daughter, Sarah, and it was agreed that if Sarah died without any children,

George would then inherit Mount Vernon. Then, when Sarah died in 1754, an arrangement was made whereby Anne leased the plantation to Washington in exchange for fifteen thousand pounds of tobacco each year. And when Anne passed away in 1760, Mount Vernon legally became Washington's property. With the passing of several family members in swift succession over a few brief years, George Washington inherited his plantation farms, the slaves that went with them, and the status of a well-to-do planter.

Originally, George Washington's Mount Vernon home was a one-and-a-half-story farmhouse with eight rooms. But over the years Washington converted it into a three-story mansion consisting of twenty-one rooms and several outbuildings, including the latrines. Slave labor was used in the tobacco fields to raise the cash crop and bring it to market, and that in turn provided Washington with the income needed to finance on-going construction projects. The exploitation of slave labor built Washington's mansion.

In 1759 Washington married Martha Dandridge Custis, a widow with two children who owned the White House plantation on the Pamunkey River near Williamsburg. She also brought to the marriage over thirty thousand dollars, and many slaves. During their first year together Martha brought about forty slaves to the Mount Vernon estate, including house slaves, tradesmen, and field slaves. She personally oversaw the work of her slaves, some of whom included Old Doll, the supervisor of work in the kitchen, Breechy, a server of food and drinks, and Betty, who performed mending work in the mansion. Washington's wealth was tied to his ownership of slaves, and his wealth increased tremendously both through marriage and inherited acquisition. Additionally, to enhance his family's business he purchased slaves throughout his lifetime and once asked West Indian dealers to buy "Negroes if choice ones be had under 40 pounds Sterling."[1]

Five farms were part of the Mount Vernon planter's domain, and he made daily inspections of each, assisting with livestock, general repairs, and building projects. The artist Janius Stearns once painted a scene depicting Washington making his rounds, dressed all in black, and performing his inspections while well-dressed slaves appeared in the painting's background. The slaves were portrayed with smiles on their faces, happily tending to Washington's fields. His farms at the time were producing eighty thousand pounds of tobacco per year.

Countless hours of hard labor went into the production of cash crops at Mount Vernon. The slaves on Washington's plantation weren't imprisoned by walls or fences, but they were concentrated together into a confined space defined by white men in power, and their movement was restricted by oppressive laws written by white legislators expressly for the maintenance of white superiority. In the colony of Virginia a law known as the "black code" stated: "It shall be unlawful for any Negro to depart from his master's ground without a pass... Violators will be dismembered." The law was meant to protect the property and wealth of planters and it certainly benefitted men like Washington. Planters could post rewards for the capture of runaway slaves, and they were legally entitled to apply the whip to the backs of black slaves if the slaves dared challenge their master's authority.[2]

One such runaway was Martha's maid, Oney Judge, who ran away from Mount Vernon and sought shelter and refuge with other free blacks. Martha thought Oney had been treated well and that the amount of work wasn't excessive. Although it was difficult for Martha to understand, Oney's resolve was so strong that it compelled her to leave Mount Vernon, and her mother and sister, to escape to freedom. Washington's friends tried to recapture Oney, but she remained free.

Another slave owned by the Washington family was Hercules, their principal cook. He fled from his master on the day that Washington left the executive office to return to Mount Vernon at the conclusion of the President's second term. Washington asked his friends to be on the lookout for Hercules, but he too was gone for good.

Not all the slaves who fled for freedom from Washington's plantations were so lucky as Oney and Hercules. Four slaves escaped in the summer of 1761, and Washington promptly posted advertisements in the newspapers of Virginia and Maryland for the return of his slaves with an offer of forty pounds sterling as the reward. According to Washington the slaves "went off without the least suspicion, provocation or difference with anybody or the least angry word or abuse from their overseers." In a written description of one slave Washington wrote, "Ran away from a plantation of the subscriber's on Dogue Run in Fairfax on Sunday the 9th instant the following slaves... Peros, 35 or 40 years of age, a well-set fellow of about 5 feet 8 inches high, yellowish complexion with a very full round face and full black beard. His speech is something slow and broke but not in so great a degree as to render him remarkable. He had on when he went a dark colour'd cloth coat, a white linen waistcoat, white breeches and white stockings." The four were all recaptured and brought back to Washington's plantation in iron chains where they were severely flogged.[3]

Washington never referred to his human property as slaves, preferring to call them "my Negroes," and "my servants," and "my people." At Mount Vernon, Washington's slaves lived in rows of one room cabins that couldn't be seen from the main house. The slave cabins had dirt floors and wooden chimneys, and they offered only the most meager shelter from the elements - little better than barn stables for farm animals. At Mount Vernon, Washington once hosted Julian Niemcewicz, a visitor from Poland, who left this description of the slave quarters at the plantation: "We entered one of the huts of the Black's, for one can not call them by the name of houses. They are more miserable than the most miserable cottages of our peasants. The husband and wife sleep on a mean pallet, the children on the ground; a very bad fireplace, some utensils for cooking, but in the middle of this poverty some cups and a teapot... A very small garden planted with vegetables was close by; with 5 or 6 hens, each one leading ten to fifteen chickens. It is the only comfort that is permitted them, for they do not keep either ducks, geese, or pigs... They work all week, not having a single day for themselves except for holidays."[4]

The slaves at Mount Vernon were given the simplest of food consisting of cornbread, a few vegetables, some pork and occasionally fish. And Washington provided only one set of new clothes to his slaves each year made of cheap cloth and linen. Overseers reported to Washington that his slaves needed more clothing and blankets and that they were frequently sick. One slave was even forced to work while he suffered from the measles. And nowhere in any of his letters did Washington show concern for the feelings of his slaves or their emotional wellbeing. Slaves provided Washington with extremely personal care, especially in cleaning his clothes, shining his boots, and cleaning out his chamber pot. And despite such intimate contact he never looked upon them as equal, or even human. They were his possessions, there to perform work for him at his command, like a horse, ox, or mule.

The master of Mount Vernon had three classes of slaves. The house servants who attended to the personal needs of George and Martha had the best existence among the slaves, with access to better clothing and food. These servants were fewer in number · perhaps only ten or eleven. Then there were the artisans, like the bakers, barrel makers, and blacksmiths, or the carpenters, masons, and tailors. These included dozens of men and women who knew specialized crafts and performed them well for the Washington family. And finally there was a third level of slaves whose lot in life was harshest of all. Their lives consisted of long hours each day working in the fields and tending to the animals. They were the ones who pulled weeds, planted new crops, brought in the harvest each season, fed the animals, and slaughtered those animals to be eaten.

At Mount Vernon, Washington forced his slaves to work hard each day, encouraging his overseers "to hurry and drive" slaves to complete their work. He instructed his managers to ensure "that my people may be at their work as soon as it is light, work till it is dark, and be diligent while they are at it." One such manager was John Alton who worked on Washington's plantation for over thirty years and managed the productivity of dozens of slaves. With the profit incentive driving Washington and his quest to accumulate greater personal wealth he pressed his slaves to improve their productivity in an effort to squeeze all that he could out of them, and he gave little thought to the miserable conditions slaves suffered in under their master's system. Washington demanded "that every laborer does as much in the 24 hours as their strength, without endangering their health, will allow."[5]

When owned by Washington a slave began working at the age of eleven, performing labor alongside adults that included plowing fields, weeding the land, and picking crops. The work was physically exhausting and slaves resented being forced to perform work for the betterment of their master. Throughout the colonies slaves rebelled in various ways, sometimes slowing down their work and stifling production. But Washington, as was the case with many other planters, threatened swift retaliation against any slaves who refused to do the work that was expected of them. Whipping the slaves was the most common form of punishment, and he once ordered an overseer named Stuart to flog a lazy field slave, directing the overseer to "give him a good whipping." And in some cases, when slaves became too unmanageable or violent, Washington sold them to sugar planters located in the West Indies, a form of punishment which usually had a tragic ending for the slaves. The severity of the punishment was not fully recognized by the slaves until they found themselves sweating in the sugar fields where many died from diseases or suffered under the most barbaric treatment at the hands of sugar plantation managers. Washington once traded away a recaptured runaway slave to the West Indies for molasses, rum, and meat.[6]

Prior to the American Revolution, Washington wrote to a friend and neighbor concerning the dire stress he felt the colonies were under at the hands of the English Parliament. In his letter he wrote, "The crisis is arrived when we must assert out rights or submit to every imposition that can be heaped upon us till custom and use shall make us as tame and abject slaves as the blacks we rule over with such arbitrary sway." Washington punished those slaves who dared to run away from him, but he was prepared to fight anyone who he thought would threaten his own freedom.[7]

Though originally a tobacco grower, Washington turned his farming efforts to the growing of apples, cherries, oats, peaches, and wheat. Mount Vernon slave labor was intensively exploited to produce ever greater varieties of products that their master demanded for increasing his profits. They had to transport and spread thousands of pounds of fertilizers, including sheep dung, in an attempt to increase the fertility of the plantation's fields. Slaves not employed in the agricultural fields often found themselves raising various animals like cows, pigs, and sheep. Some slaves became specialists, like butchers, and learned how to cure meat in smoke houses. Other specialists included Washington's spinners, usually women, who performed the work needed to turn wool into thread, and then thread into cloth. There were also lumberjacks who cut trees and transformed the wood into the boards used in the construction of many of Mount Vernon's buildings.

Slaves performed all these types of jobs in the service of their master, yet Washington, in a letter written to Robert Morris, once wrote, "I can only say that there is not a man living who wishes more sincerely than I do to see a plan adopted for the abolition" of slavery. These were his words, yet he owned slaves, and everything about his lifestyle and his position in society depended upon the work of his slaves. In 1787 Washington declared, "Nothing but the rooting out of slavery can perpetuate the existence of our union by consolidating it in a common bond of principle." Washington repeated the belief a dozen years later in a similar statement when he met with the English actor John Bernard who recalled Washington saying, "I can clearly foresee that nothing but the rooting out of slavery" can save the Union. Though he shared thoughts such as these both publicly and privately, Washington never pressed for the abolishment of slavery from the republic. The most respected leader in America never stood up for the freedom and liberty of the people in his country who were most in need of it. The warrior who led armies into battle, and survived the violence and bloodshed of war, refused to fight a political battle on behalf of the enslaved portion of the American democracy.[8]

Finally, near the end of his life, Washington put into writing the words that were to free his slaves. His will directed that his slaves were to go free after Martha died, and that they be given some education so that they could survive as free people in a country where most black people were slaves. Of America's founding fathers that owned slaves, Washington was the only one who granted them their freedom. A community of over 120 people formerly belonging to Washington were freed. Martha's own slaves were to be given their freedom upon her death, though legally they were the property of the Custis heirs. With the prospects of her slaves' freedom hinging upon her life, Martha lived the last years of her life believing that her slaves wanted her to die.[9]

"Tom" from Mount Vernon. (Ambrotype ca. 1861-65)

"Life of George Washington – the Farmer." Painted by J. B. Stearns, 1853. Library of Congress, copy-free public domain.

Empowered by Slavery

two

Thomas Jefferson's Monticello

Empowered by Slavery

Chapter 2: Thomas Jefferson's Monticello

In the state of Virginia, not far from the Rivanna River, on top of a mountain, a masterfully designed mansion was erected, with numerous unseen living quarters located close by for the slaves who served their master by sweating in his fields and providing the labor required to create and sustain his tremendous wealth. The master of these slaves was also, during the course of his life, the president and founder of the University of Virginia. He served as George Washington's secretary of state, and was vice president during the administration of John Adams. He authored the Declaration of Independence, and was the third President of the United States. Thomas Jefferson was all of these things, and the name of the slave plantation he called home was Monticello.

Jefferson's mansion was built brick by brick, in a labor system similar to that of the Spanish missions of California. In fact, the Franciscan padres were making use of Native Californian labor in the construction of their missionary compounds when Jefferson's overseers were driving the black slave labor used to erect Monticello. The physical structures at both locations depended heavily on the making of bricks. In California, the padres were concerned with building massive structures that could support religious functions, ceremonies, and symbolism, as well as provide homes and shelter for the Spanish colonists and the native people who lived in the mission communities. The padres' bricks were adobe - a mixture of mud and straw that was dried in the sun. They were easy and inexpensive to make, and they were usually functional rather than aesthetic. The bricks made at Monticello, on the other hand, were a product of industry, with an eye for the aesthetic. Jefferson's slaves made many thousands of bricks, all fire-hardened in ovens for extra strength and durability. Their master was intent on building something that could last for many decades.

In the use of bricks Jefferson had a cheap but durable building material. Though inexpensive, bricks did require Jefferson to employ the services of a brick maker who had the knowledge needed to create the quality Jefferson desired for Monticello. One such person was a white man named George Dudley who was assisted by many black slaves in the making of Jefferson's bricks. White brick layers and carpenters on slave plantations such as Monticello were each supported by a few black slaves who did the hardest and most labor intensive physical work. Part of the brick making process required combining limestone with sand, and this was usually performed by the slaves, a difficult and dirty chore that contributed to respiratory illnesses and health problems.

In their support of the carpenters, slaves performed all the heavy lifting and difficult labor, which included cutting down trees, sawing lumber, and lifting, carrying, and transporting materials into position for use and installation. Monticello became a life-long architectural project for Jefferson, one in which his home was constantly in some state of construction. There was always a goal for its completion in mind, but it wasn't to be realized until near the end of Jefferson's life. Slaves who spent much of their lives confined to work at Monticello either worked directly on the construction efforts, or they were utilized in the fields and industries that helped to support their master. Some slaves worked to raise horses, while others spent many hours of their lives making nails, and the horses and nails produced in Jefferson's industrial efforts were marketed and sold to support Monticello.

The nail-making business Jefferson initiated at Monticello was one enterprise in which the master spent a greater amount of time with his slaves. He seemed unwilling to spend time behind the plow himself or to keep watch over the slaves in his fields, but his nail industry was of keen interest to him. Beginning at the age of ten and lasting until their sixteenth year, many of the young boys that Jefferson owned were employed in his nail shop where they labored away from the early morning hours until late in the day. Those unfortunate adolescents suffered through twelve long hours of tedious work that was repetitive and boring, and Jefferson monitored the performance of each slave boy, tracking how many nails they could produce each day, and how efficient they were in their use of materials. He noted wastage and streamlined operations. Of his young slaves Jefferson once wrote, "from 10 to 16, the boys to make nails, the girls spin."[10]

Making nails was among the worst jobs that slaves were commanded to do as it was a mindless process, machine-like in orientation, and repetitive in its drudgery. The nail-making system would regularly break down due to Jefferson's frequent and lengthy absences from Monticello. When Jefferson was away, and no overseer was around to monitor work, slave boys would simply slack off in their production of nails. But Jefferson, like most large plantation owners, hired overseers that strictly enforced the labor system.

On one occasion, one of Jefferson's young slaves, Cary, violently attacked another young slave, named Brown. Both were nail makers, and the nature of the violent attack was so extreme that it might easily have ended in the death of Brown. When Jefferson learned of the trouble in one of his most important industries he ordered that the guilty party be removed from the nail shop, that he be imprisoned, and that he not be allowed to talk to anyone or be seen by any of the other slaves. Then Jefferson ordered that the slave be sold to some place far away, writing that "it would be to the others as if he were put out of the way by death." Jefferson didn't want to order the death of one of his slaves as punishment for a violent crime, but he made it appear that capital punishment was a possibility for any slave who dared to resort to violent behavior.[11]

In the past the word "benevolent" was used to describe Jefferson as a slave holder, especially in comparison to other plantation owners of Jefferson's day. Jefferson's "benevolence" was based on his management style, one in which he preferred to sell slaves away from his plantations rather than resort to corporal or capital punishment. But slaves at Monticello couldn't always count on such benevolence. Among the overseers that Jefferson employed was Gabriel Lilly who made use of the whip to force and coerce labor from the slaves until Jefferson finally put a stop to it. "It would destroy their value in my estimation to degrade them in their own eyes by the whip," Jefferson wrote. "This therefore must not be resorted to but in extremities. As they will be again under my government, I would chuse they should retain the stimulus of character." Jefferson therefore disliked the idea of whipping human beings, but he admitted that it might be resorted to if he felt it was necessary.[12]

Jamey Hubbard, one man among Jefferson's many slaves, ran away from his master's plantation when he decided freedom was worth such a risk. However, he was captured and forcibly returned to his master. But undeterred, Hubbard ran away again, only to be captured once again. He was brought back to his master in iron chains. As punishment for the sin he committed of seeking his freedom he was severely flogged. With the whip having been applied to his back, and with the sting and pain of that whip still fresh in his mind, Hubbard ran away again because he refused to surrender his will to be free.

Another instance of slave rebellion and subsequent punishment occurred at Jefferson's Bedford plantation when a slave named Billy stabbed an overseer and was then sentenced to be burned on the hand and whipped. Throughout the colonial period, and well into the early years of the young republic, the overseers employed in American plantations could be brutal in their treatment of slaves, and those found at Monticello were no exception. An additional example is found in the story of James Hemings, a nail shop slave who was severely beaten by the overseer Gabriel Lilly. Jefferson's carpenter, James Oldham, described the beating of Hemings in chilling detail, noting "the barbarity that he maid use of with little Jimmy was the moost cruel." Lilly had beaten Hemings with the whip three times in a single day. Slaves were also supervised by black men that Jefferson referred to as "headmen" in his writings, and these men were rewarded in their efforts to keep other slaves on task with preferential treatment from their master.[13]

Jefferson, unwilling to wholeheartedly resort to the threat of violence that the master-slave relationship implied, considered alternative ways to encourage his slaves to be productive in their work. He allowed slaves to plant their own gardens, instilling in them a sense of empowerment and ownership in their work and lives. Though most of their waking hours were managed by their masters, the slaves of Monticello usually had at least one day each week to spend at their own discretion. They were free to use their time in leisurely pursuits or to tend to their own plots of Monticello's grounds in which their vegetable gardens grew. The simplistic diet Jefferson served to his slaves, the main staple of which was a flat loaf of corn meal, certainly encouraged slaves to find additional ways to supplement the food they ate. In addition to gardens, slaves on Jefferson's plantations sometimes raised their own poultry and swine, or they caught fish in local streams and ponds.

Though he was a master who placed heavy physical demands on his slaves, Jefferson was also concerned with the health and welfare of his labor force and he frequently cared for those who were too sick, old, or unable to work. Of men held by the chains of bondage Jefferson once wrote, "feed and clothe them well, protect them from ill usage, require such reasonable labor only as is performed voluntarily by freemen." While the language has an enlightened ring to it, the truth was that the performance of labor at Monticello wasn't voluntary, and the master wasn't about to test whether the men and women he owned would voluntarily stay and perform such work for him if they were freed.[14]

Thomas Jefferson's whole existence, from the days of his early childhood when he learned the practices and procedures of managing his father's slave population, to the final days of his life when he reigned as the patriarch of his family and the sage of Monticello, depended on the legality of slavery and the institution's ability to extract forced labor from captive people and convert it into wealth. The ownership of human beings was a business interest of Jefferson, and he both bought and sold slaves throughout his life. He even sold one person for six hundred dollars while serving as the nation's executive officer, and he frequently rented slaves for his own projects, or loaned them out to other planters. His entire status in society, the independence he enjoyed, and the experimental projects he pursued in the world of science, were only possible because scores of slaves labored to build and sustain his wealth and status.

Peter Jefferson, Thomas' father, passed away when Thomas Jefferson was still young. In passing, Peter left to his family ownership of sixty slaves. In the year 1769, seven years before the American states declared their independence from Britain, Thomas Jefferson counted fifty-two "proper slaves" in his Farm Book. Three years later, in 1772, Jefferson's marriage to Martha Skelton brought an additional 135 slaves to the Jefferson plantations. In the late 1790s Jefferson's slave population fluctuated upwards to approximately two hundred people. With all of his business interests, including vast construction projects and his own penchant for wanting to lavishly care for guests, Jefferson ran up large debts during his life, and when the creditors came to collect it sometimes forced Jefferson to sell some of his slaves. In one ten year period he sold over 160 slaves in order to pay down the amount of money that he owed. But still, with natural population increases alone, the number of slaves that Jefferson owned remained high - well above one hundred and very close to two hundred through most of his life. In all, Thomas Jefferson came to own seven plantations. His farm sites went by the names Shadwell, Tufton, Poplar Forest, Bear Creek, Lego, Tomahawk, and Monticello. Each was a camp of concentrated, enforced labor.

The lives of Jefferson's house slaves were marginally better than those of the people slaving away in the fields of Monticello. They had access to better food and drink and generally enjoyed better living conditions. But they were in subservient positions and forced to live their lives knowing they had little control over their destinies. One such house slave, Jupiter, had perhaps one of the closest relationships a slave could have with the master of Monticello, but that didn't prevent him from being forced to perform difficult and dangerous work blasting and hauling limestone for construction projects. And when Jefferson went to France, Jupiter was hired out to perform labor for others that earned money for his master.

Though Monticello was built on a foundation of slave labor, part of Jefferson's genius devoted itself to concealing that fact from guests, family members, and even from Jefferson himself. The master of the plantation spent a great amount of time designing and redesigning the architectural plans for his mountaintop home, and he consciously concealed certain sections by creating separate buildings for the kitchen activities, for the laundering needs, for his stable of animals, and for the privy. He wanted to keep the sights, sounds, and smells of the daily work performed by his slaves hidden from the place where he entertained guests, where he read and wrote, and where he slept and ate. And the slaves' quarters were usually among the buildings farthest from the Monticello mansion. Some of these were located along a series of mulberry trees that came to be known as Mulberry Row. The living conditions of Jefferson's slaves changed over time, just as the mansion building itself changed. Small log cabins were called home by many of his slaves, though some slaves later lived in shelters made of brick. A 1796 insurance policy described slave quarters at Monticello as being made of "wood, with a wooden chimney, the floor earth." Other descriptions of slave quarters at Monticello referred to a continuous structure made of brick that was built into the side of the hill and divided into one room cabins. A series of subterranean passageways were built that allowed slaves to pass undetected by people in the mansion. These lower halls and tunnels were designed by Jefferson to make his slaves almost invisible.[15]

Although Jefferson hired white laborers to work on his construction projects at Monticello, the majority of people working at the plantation were black, and they were the ones who dug the earth, hammered things together, built things up, and tore other things down. They made mountains of bricks, and then they moved those bricks to where they were needed, lifting, carrying, and placing individual bricks into place. Monticello occupied a visually spectacular location, and it was blessed with clay-based soil that was perfect for the making of bricks. But the plantation's location on top of a mountain left it with limited access to water, and this meant the slaves had to transport the water from lower regions. Additionally, these difficult working conditions were exacerbated by Jefferson when he directed his slaves to dig into the side of the mountain and flatten out a large plateau in which cash crops like wheat and tobacco could be grown. The natural and rugged terrain of a mountain was transformed into an artificially constructed environment by the use of forced human labor to satisfy the needs of a single man. Raw human energy reshaped the landscape according to

Jefferson's designs. The slaves who did the work had no choice in the matter. They were simply directed by Jefferson's overseers as instructed by the master. Slaves who were confined to Monticello were embedded in a larger system that exploited concentrated labor. The institution of slavery was legal prior to the American colonies declaring their independence, and it continued to be legal after the states formed a new nation, because it was deeply embedded in the culture and civilization and it significantly fueled the power and wealth that men like Jefferson enjoyed.

Thomas Jefferson, as the author of the Declaration of Independence, struggled throughout his lifetime to justify ownership of slaves even while he frequently admitted that slavery was an evil that had to be abolished. He once wrote, "The whole commerce between master and slave is a perpetual exercise of the most boisterous passions, the most unremitting despotism on the one part, and degrading submissions on the other... The man must be a prodigy who can retain his manners and morals undepraved by such circumstances." Time and again he made such admissions in his writings. In his original draft of the Declaration he argued that the King of England "waged cruel war against human nature itself, violating its most sacred rights of life and liberty in the persons of a distant people who never offended him, captivating and carrying them into slavery in another hemisphere, or to incur miserable death in their transportation thither." What Jefferson wrote was true enough in the sense that England was responsible for transporting black slaves to the Americas, but it was hypocritical for Jefferson to charge others of such a sin when he himself exploited black labor for his own good. These words from his first draft proved too controversial for other American rebel leaders so they were removed from the final version of the Declaration. In explaining the deletion Jefferson noted, "the clause too, reprobating the enslaving the inhabitants of Africa, was struck out in complaisance to South Carolina and Georgia, who had never attempted to restrain the importation of slaves, and who on the contrary still wished to continue it."[16]

Later in his life, within the content of his autobiography, Jefferson wrote, "Nothing is more certainly written in the book of fate than that these people are to be free; nor is it less certain, that the two races, equally free, cannot live in the same government. Nature, habit, opinion has drawn indelible lines of distinction between them. It is still in our power to direct the process of emancipation and deportation, peaceably, and in such slow degree, as that the evil will wear off insensibly." These seventy-four words written by the hand of Jefferson are perhaps the best example of the nature of the conflict that existed in the hearts, minds, and souls of many of America's founding fathers, and they especially serve to illustrate Jefferson's own personal ethical struggle with the institution. When he said that nothing is more certain than that black people were meant to be free he provided a correct prophecy for the future of the country. But despite his incredible intellect, Jefferson failed to think it was possible that black people could stand and contribute equally in the American democracy, a deficiency rooted in his own racist and discriminatory views of non-whites. Of black people he wrote that he believed them to be "inferior to the whites in the endowments both of body and mind...unfortunate difference of colour, and perhaps of faculty is a powerful obstacle to the emancipation of these people." In arguing that nature has drawn indelible lines, Jefferson's discriminatory thinking attempted to justify white superiority over black people through his own scientific understanding of the natural world. His mind was always geared toward organizing things into a logical order. And when he expressed his belief that black people should be both emancipated and deported from America it was the chilling conclusion he drew for terminating the evil institution. Sending the slaves back to Africa, or some other acceptable location, was his solution, and he hoped that it could be done without conflict or violence in a way that would simply leave the wrongs of the past to be forgotten over time.[17]

The racist beliefs that allowed Jefferson to serve as the master of slave plantations also shaped his opinion concerning future scenarios if black people were emancipated. In his Notes on the State of Virginia, Jefferson framed the freedom question, and then answered it by expressing his fears. "Why not retain and incorporate the blacks into the State, and thus save the expence of supplying, by importation of white settlers, the vacancies they will leave?" he asked. "Deep-rooted prejudices entertained by the whites; ten thousand recollections, by the blacks, of the injuries they have sustained; new provocations; the real distinctions which nature has made; and many other circumstances, will divide us into parties, and produce convulsions, which will probably never end but in the extermination of the one or the other race," he answered. In a letter to Jared Sparks written in 1824 he expressed similar concerns stating, "there are in the United States a million and a half people of color in slavery. To send off the whole of these at once, nobody conceives to be practicable for us, or expedient for them. Let us take twenty-five years for its accomplishment."[18]

Jefferson, as a planter, used his intellect to improve the value of his holdings through intense analysis and the constant refinement of how his operations were run. Of slaves he once wrote, "I know of no error more consuming to an estate than that of stocking farms with men almost exclusively. I consider a woman who brings a child every two years as more profitable than the best men of the farm. What she produces is an addition to capital, while his labors disappear in mere consumption." In other words, owning slaves, and encouraging their reproduction for sale on the market, is where the money was.[19]

A general fear of slave rebellion gripped Jefferson and other planters throughout the republic in its early years. "The spirit of the master is abating, that of the slave rising from the dust, his condition mollifying," wrote Jefferson, "the way I hope preparing, under the auspices of heaven, for a total emancipation, and that this is disposed, in the order of events, to be with the consent of the masters, rather than by their extirpation." Jefferson believed that the owners of slaves should find some way to free the men and women that they held in bondage before forces that they couldn't hope to control utterly destroyed them. You will change, he argued, if you know what's good for you.[20]

Racism, however, was a more powerful force than reason. Planters such as Jefferson lived too much of their lives in the belief that the black people living among them were not equal, and perhaps not even fully human. Black people of Jefferson's time were regarded as little better than beasts of burden. If they were free black people, then they were still looked down upon by the white majority in America as unfortunate, lesser beings. On the subject of possible intermarriage between black and white people Jefferson once argued that it "produces a degradation to which no lover of his country, no lover of excellence in the human character can innocently consent."[21]

The evils of the institution of slavery were well known to Jefferson, but he lived his life from beginning to end within the wealthy comfort provided by the forced labor of his family's black slaves. "Indeed I tremble for my country when I reflect that God is just: that his justice cannot sleep forever: that considering numbers, nature, and natural means only, a revolution of the wheel of fortune, an exchange of situation, is among possible events," he wrote. And, in an 1820 letter to John Holmes, Jefferson pondered, "This momentous question [slavery], like a fire bell in the night, awakened and filled me with terror. I consider it at once as the knell of the Union." In

1784 Jefferson proposed to prohibit slavery west of the Alleghenies, but failed in Congress. Losing by one vote Jefferson commented, "Thus we see the fate of millions unborn hanging on the tongue of one man, and heaven was silent in that awful moment!" In 1800 President Jefferson failed in his attempt to inaugurate the deportation of blacks to distant colonies. Years later, he died without freeing his slaves in his will, and many were sold to pay down his debts. And the civil war he feared would happen, as a result of slavery's infestation of America, did happen.[22]

"Inspection and Sale of a Negro." Whitney engraving, 1854. Library of Congress, copy-free public domain.

Monticello, home of President Thomas Jefferson.

Empowered by Slavery

three

James Madison's Montpelier

Empowered by Slavery

Chapter 3: James Madison's Montpelier

The fourth President of the United States was another of the republic's founding fathers, and a principal author of America's Constitution. He served as a colonel in the militia, he was an elected delegate at Virginia's Constitutional Convention, and he served as Thomas Jefferson's secretary of state. His was a long and distinguished political career, and in 1808 it was crowned by winning a majority of votes cast by citizens of the United States for the country's highest office. Yet he owed much of his success to the vast wealth generated by his family's ownership of black slaves.

James Madison, Jr. was born in March of 1751 at Port Conway. He was the first of his parents' twelve children, only seven of whom survived to adulthood. As a child he spent time in boarding school, and in home-schooling with instruction provided by Reverend Thomas Martin. The education he received prepared him for academic studies at the College of New Jersey at Princeton where he studied Greek, Latin, science, philosophy, math, and logic. When he completed his college education he returned to his family's home, the plantation known as Montpelier, where he continued his personal studies of law and government even as he suffered from ill health. Montpelier was the home he was born and raised in. As the oldest son of James, Sr., Madison inherited Montpelier when his father passed away in February of 1801.

James Madison became the owner of five thousand acres of plantation farmland between the Southwest Mountains and the Rapidan in Orange County, Virginia. The core of the plantation's mansion was constructed in the 1760s, when Madison was still a child, and he retained memories of helping to move small items from the family's old house to their new one. His father had been the largest slave owner in the county and as such his duties included serving as the chief fiscal officer, the dispenser of punishments, and the commander of the militia. James, Jr. was expected to follow in his father's footsteps and manage the plantation, which was the surest method of maintaining the family's wealth and status in society.

Like George Washington and Thomas Jefferson, James Madison inherited his wealth. He was born into a rich family, and in comparison to most people living in the colonies during his time, Madison was tremendously wealthy. Status symbols adorned the Madison home. A woman named Mary Cutts once described the Montpelier mansion as having within its walls Persian rugs and Parisian statuary. The walls were said to be "covered with mirrors and pictures," and there were paintings by master artists. Madison's mansion had mahogany tables, alabaster vases, and sideboards loaded with silver. There were chests full of cutlery, sugar bowls, and wine glasses. The mantle was made of marble and the windows were covered with silk drapes. And in Madison's study room he had a fine desk and chairs, along with Marie Antoinette's china. His collection of books included classics, and books on science, philosophy, poetry, and traveling. And Madison could also produce for his guests an original copy of the Declaration of Independence.[23]

Outside the mansion Ms. Cutts took notice of "immense waving fields of grain" and tobacco. There were trees planted all around the mansion including mulberry, willow, and pine. And Madison also grew fruit trees such as apples, pears, and plums next to beds of strawberries.

The oldest section of Montpelier was constructed around 1764 by James Madison, Sr. When it was completed, the home was the largest brick building in Orange County, a testament to the family's wealth, status, and position within colonial America. The plantation mansion that James Madison, Jr. inherited was a home that underwent multiple renovations through the years, much like Thomas Jefferson's Monticello. During the mansion's first years it consisted of a two-story brick house with four rooms on the first floor, a cellar, and five living spaces on the second floor. In 1797 James, Jr. added thirty feet of new brick construction to the northeast side of the house in order to provide a separate living space for himself and his wife Dolley. And then a large portico was added to the front of the house to unify the new additions with older portions. An insurance policy issued by the Mutual Assurance Society of Richmond in 1799 noted that the house was thirty-three feet by eighty-six feet, two stories tall, and worth about six thousand dollars. Madison continued to add on to the mansion through the years, increasing the home's size as his wealth and power increased. New wing cellars were constructed with each wing having its own kitchen, and this meant cooking was done inside the house for the first time. Montpelier slaves previously cooked food for the Madison's in a separate brick kitchen located to the south of the mansion. They would then bring food into the home to the Madison's dining table.

A woman named Mrs. Smith once visited Montpelier and was served wine and pineapples by the slaves. "Hospitality is the presiding genius of the house," declared Mrs. Smith, "and Mrs. M. is kindness personified." Mrs. Smith spent the night with the Madison's in their mansion and then had breakfast with them the next morning on a gazebo where black slaves served white diners an assortment of meats including chicken and ham, and a variety of cakes, hash, wheat bread, corn, coffee, and tea. "Freedom" was the word Mrs. Smith used to describe James Madison's Montpelier slave plantation.[24]

Many other words could've been used by the black slaves to describe conditions they experienced at the home of America's fourth President. While guests of the Madisons' dined on pineapples and fine wine, slaves could expect little more than corn and potatoes for the bulk of their diet. During the Madisons' ownership of the Montpelier estate, five or more generations lived and worked at the plantation, and they exceeded a hundred in number. The vast majority of these people lived in small one room cabins made of logs, stones, or bricks, with earth floors. James Madison's grandfather, Ambrose Madison, originally laid claim to the land in 1723 and the first people to live there were Amrbose's slaves who were forced to clear the land, prepare it for construction projects and farming, and erect the first home for the Madison family, known as Mount Pleasant. At the time of Amrbose's death he owned twenty-nine slaves. After his passing, the family continued to enslave these men, women, and children. And the Madison's furthered the scope of their plantation by increasing the number of their slaves. James Madison, Sr. had one of the largest plantations in Orange County, and its success was entirely dependent on slave labor. White slave owners like the Madisons passed along their wealth, in the form of human chattel, from one generation to the next. Black slave workers couldn't pass along anything to their descendants, and generation after generation they suffered the same redundancy, the same monotony, and the same drudgery as their predecessors.

James Madison, Sr. sought ways to diversify and expand upon his plantation's productivity, and he broadened the number of crops his slaves tended to by introducing corn, rye, wheat, and hemp to his fields. His efforts met with success and the formula he used to increase his wealth called for reinvesting his profits into more land, and more slaves to work that land. When James Madison, Sr., died in 1801 he bequeathed to his family ownership of 108 slaves. This was close to the number that President James Madison maintained throughout his lifetime.

Of these many slaves that the Madison family owned, most were used as field hands, tending to the farms and raising the crops that the Montpelier plantation depended upon for its existence. A smaller number were assigned the work of specialists, people who developed specialized skills such as blacksmiths, wagon drivers, millers, and weavers. Others were carpenters and brick makers, or distillers of brandy and whisky, or sawmill workers. And when their skills weren't being put to use at Montpelier, the slaves could expect to be loaned out for work at other colonial plantations.

Of all Madison's slaves, a small number tended to the Madison family's personal needs. There were slaves who were cooks, and those who were gardeners. Slaves performed the roles of maids and butlers, and a select few served as personal servants of James, Jr. and Dolley. When Madison attended the College of New Jersey in Princeton, for example, he took with him a personal servant by the name of Sawney, and so trusted did Sawney become to the Madisons that they depended upon him for the rest of his life. Sawney's efforts earned him an overseer position on part of the Montpelier plantation.

In 1807 a British diplomat by the name of Sir Augustus Foster visited Madison at Montpelier and later provided this account of his experience at the plantation: "His house stands upon the Southwest Mountains... It is of brick... Mr. Madison has about ten or twelve hundred acres of land at this place which is called Montpelier, and as, from his situation in the republic, he was obliged to be often absent from home, he was under the necessity of trusting to his overseer a great deal... Mr. Madison assured me that after providing for this overseer, clothing his Negroes, and deducting the expences for repairs, the profits which he derived from the estate did not exceed the overseer's pay... The Negro habitations are separate from the dwelling house both here and all over Virginia, and they form a kind of village as each Negro family would like... At Montpelier I found a forge, a turner's shop, a carpenter, and wheelwright... The slaves, however, are unwilling to make their own clothes, and during the Revolutionary War, it was very difficult to get them to spin or to card wool... The Negro women too preferred a great deal working in the fields to spinning and sewing. They appeared to me to be a happy thoughtless race of people when under a kind master as was the Secretary of State." Madison tried to convince the diplomat that the life of a slave owning planter was not one of wealth and luxury, and that he profited little more than the white overseers he employed. But it's certainly not likely that the overseers were able to afford the finer things in life, such as a collection of Marie Antoinette's china.[25]

Another visitor to Madison's Montpelier estate was the Harvard professor George Ticknor who visited the Madisons in 1824 and left this account of the plantation: "On Sunday forenoon we took a ride of a dozen miles across different plantations, to see the country and the people. Mr. Madison's farm - as he calls it - consists of about three thousand acres, with an hundred and eighty slaves, and is among the best managed in Virginia." White visitors to the Madison estate were for the most part deeply impressed by the hospitality shown to them by the Madison family, and they frequently mentioned the service provided to them by the planter's many servants.[26]

The servants themselves left accounts of their experiences working for the Madison family. Among the slaves at the Montpelier plantation was a man named Paul Jennings who was born in 1799 when Madison was forty-eight years old. As a young child Jennings accompanied Madison to Washington D.C. when the fourth President was sworn into office. "When Mr. Madison was chosen President, we came on and moved into the White House," Jennings remembered years later. "The east room was not finished, and Pennsylvania Avenue was not paved, but was always in an awful condition from either dust or mud. The city was a dreary place." Jennings remained a servant to Madison to the end of the President's life.[27]

During his time with Madison in Washington D.C., Jennings played a vital role in the salvation of George Washington's portrait during the War of 1812 when British soldiers burned down the White House. Jennings and Dolley Madison rescued the painting by the artist Landsowne just before soldiers torched the executive mansion. The portrait can now be seen in the East Room of the White House thanks in part to the efforts of Paul Jennings.

After Madison's two terms in office Jennings returned with his master to the Montpelier plantation, and he continued to serve as Madison's personal manservant until Madison's final day. "I was always with Mr. Madison till he died," wrote Jennings. "For six months before his death, he was unable to walk, and spent most of his time reclined on a couch; but his mind was bright, and with his numerous visitors he talked with as much animation and strength of voice as I ever heard him in his best days. I was present when he died. That morning Sukey brought him breakfast, as usual. He could not swallow. His niece, Mrs. Willis, said, 'What is the matter, uncle James?' 'Nothing more than a change of mind, my dear.' His head instantly dropped, and he ceased breathing as quietly as the snuff of a candle goes out. He was about eighty-four years old, and was followed to the grave by an immense procession of white and colored people." That a large number of Madison's slaves attended the funeral of their master suggests that Madison was among the most benign of slave owning founding fathers.[28]

Slaves at Montpelier were housed and fed better than other slaves found almost anywhere else in America. Madison saw slaves as human beings, not as chattel. To Mordecai Collins, one of Madison's overseers employed at the Broad Meadows farm, Madison directed that slaves should be provided "with all the humanity and kindness consistent with their necessary subordination and work." Madison never struck a slave, nor did he give permission to overseers to use such violent methods against the workers.[29]

Still, the black people who lived at the Montpelier plantation were confined to its space, and were forced to work from dawn until dusk, in good weather or bad, in the rain and snow, and on the hottest and most humid days of the year. Slaves worked for Madison six days a week, and they only had Sundays off for themselves to either rest and relax, or care for their own personal gardens where they grew vegetables like cabbages and sweet potatoes. Some used their free time to fish or hunt small game like squirrels and rabbits.

After Madison's death Dolley and the family began to have difficulties managing the plantation and this led to financial troubles. In a will that Dolley composed in 1841 she wrote, "I give to my mulatto man Paul his freedom." But Jennings had reason to believe that the future's promised freedom was threatened by the rapidly dwindling wealth Dolley possessed towards the end of her life. In 1846 Dolley sold Jennings to an insurance agent named Pollard Webb, apparently ending Jennings' chance at freedom. But then Senator Daniel Webster purchased Jennings six months later and guaranteed his freedom in exchange for a short-term labor agreement. "I have paid $120 for the freedom of Paul Jennings," wrote Webster. "He agrees to work out the same at $8/month, to be furnished with board, clothes, washing... his freedom papers I gave to him." Towards the end of Dolley Madison's life, Paul Jennings offered assistance to his former owner. "Mrs. Madison was a remarkable woman," Jennings wrote. "She was beloved by every body in Washington, white and colored... In the last days of her life, before Congress purchased her husband's papers, she was in a state of absolute poverty, and I think sometimes suffered for the necessaries of life. While I was a servant of Mr. Webster, he often sent me to her with a market-basket full of provisions, and told me whenever I saw anything in the house that I thought was in need of, to take it to her. I often did this, and occasionally gave her small sums from my own pocket, though I had years before bought my freedom of her."[30]

James Madison, and several other founding fathers, including Thomas Jefferson and George Washington, made statements during the course of their lives in which they expressed their regret over the existence of slavery. They knew that slavery was wrong and that it was an evil that needed to end. At the Constitutional Convention Madison reported, "Every master of slaves is born a petty tyrant." Yet planters like Madison also believed they couldn't free their slaves for fear that they wouldn't be able to survive as free people living in a society dominated by whites. It was racial bigotry within the best of men. And proof that these plantation owners were wrong in their thinking was supplied by a former slave of Madison's. George Gilmore was emancipated at the end of the Civil War after living for fifty years as a Montpelier slave. He started his own farm one mile from the plantation. Gilmore and his wife, Polly, built a cabin on the remains of a Confederate camp in the 1870s, and they were successful farmers. Gilmore officially purchased the sixteen acres in 1901 from Dr. James A. Madison, a great-nephew of President Madison, and he died four years later at the age of ninety-five. Gilmore was proof that freed slaves could be successful and live productive lives.[31]

Madison and the other founding fathers, however, weren't alive to witness the emancipation of the nation's slaves. During Madison's life he spent a considerable amount of time thinking and writing about slavery, and he pondered the possibility of abolishing it by shipping black slaves to Africa. A solution to the slavery problem that Madison endorsed focused on the federal government shipping all of America's slaves to Africa and paying for it by selling America's western lands acquired in the Louisiana Purchase. In Madison's letter to Robert Evans in June, 1819, he defined some of the mathematical details:

"If slavery as a national evil is to be abolished, and it be just that it be done at the national expence, the amount of the expence is not a paramount consideration. It is the peculiar fortune, or rather a providential blessing of the U.S. to possess a resource commensurate to this great object, without taxes on the people, or even an increase of the Public debt... I allude to the vacant territory the extent to which is so vast, and the vendible value of which is so well ascertained... This will require 200 Mils. of acres at 3 dolrs. per acre; or 300 Mills. at 2 dollrs. per acre a quantity, which tho' great in itself, is perhaps not a third part of the disposable territory belonging to the U.S." Thus, Madison's financial solution to the slavery problem was to be solved by sale of public land. The United States claimed ownership of the Louisiana Territory because the U.S. had purchased it from France. Of course all the Native Americans living within the territory objected to the notion that others owned the land their communities had lived on for countless generations. Madison endeavored to remove black people from North America by shipping them back to Africa, and at the same time he referred to Native American land as "vacant territory." Racial prejudice caused white Americans to view Native Americans as something less than human and to regard them as unworthy possessors of the land. Ultimately, white Americans believed that their own progress depended on removing non-whites from the land.[32]

In 1835 the English author Harriet Martineau visited Montpelier and wrote about Madison's concerns regarding slavery: "He talked more on the subject of slavery than on any other, acknowledging, without limitation or hesitation, all the evils with which it has ever been charged." Despite knowing that slavery was wrong, Madison failed to find a solution for ridding the institution from the nation he helped to create. Nor did he come to the conclusion that he should personally free his own slaves because he convinced himself that they would be worse off without him. With him as their master, he believed, they would at least be well fed and well clothed.

Among Montpelier's barns, plows, smokehouses, and timber lands were the quarters of the slaves. None of Montpelier's farms, the five thousand productive acres, the pastures, fields, and orchards, and none of the physical structures, from the mansion to the simplest of outbuildings, would have been possible without the use of forced human labor provided by generations of black people who worked long and hard in the service of their master. Madison couldn't see the way to true freedom for all people because with true freedom the life he knew and enjoyed would not exist.[33]

"America," by E. W. Clay, published 1841. "Idealized portrayal of American slavery." Library of Congress, copy-free public domain.

"James Madison, fourth President of the United States," by G. Stuart, 1828. Library of Congress, copy-free public domain.

Empowered by Slavery

four

Andrew Jackson's Hermitage

Empowered by Slavery

Chapter 4: Andrew Jackson's Hermitage

The American President Andrew Jackson was another wealthy slave owning planter from the South, following in the tradition of George Washington, Thomas Jefferson, and James Madison. He was part of the next generation of political giants in the United States. Jackson was born to poor Irish immigrants in the year 1767, near Camden in South Carolina. While too young to participate in the war for American independence, Jackson wasn't too young to have the impact of that struggle hit close to home. The conflict claimed the lives of his brothers, and these were among the first tragedies in a life marked repeatedly by violent confrontations and political battles.

As a young man, Jackson studied law. He became a lawyer, and then a judge. He was elected to local political offices, and he served his country in the Army. He led soldiers into battles, and gained fame in the War of 1812 by defeating the British at New Orleans. The commission he earned in the armed forces, and the money he earned working in law were stepping stones towards Jackson's accumulation of a great fortune. He used his money to buy land and slaves and he became a prosperous southern planter. The work performed by his slaves in the fields brought in ever greater wealth, and Jackson reinvested his profits, purchasing even more acreage and human capital. After living at his Poplar Grove plantation in the early 1790s, and then at his Hunter's Hill plantation until 1804, Jackson purchased land from Nathaniel Hays that was to become the Hermitage for $3400. Twelve miles outside of Nashville, this 425 acre farm was the final home and principal slave plantation of Andrew Jackson.

At first the Hermitage was a collection of log cabins, and it was in a two-story farmhouse that Jackson's family lived until 1821 when work was completed on a larger brick mansion. The original farmhouse was given to the slaves when their master moved into his mansion. The

Hermitage plantation buildings included a log duplex building that served as the kitchen and additional housing for the slaves who prepared the meals. The kitchen was located forty feet from Jackson's original residence. Just like Jefferson's Monticello, the slaves who prepared their master's meals at Jackson's Hermitage were required to do so outside of the main residence building.

The Hermitage plantation grew in complexity over time. There were carriage houses, stables, barns, a carpenter's shop, a greenhouse, an icehouse, and a smokehouse in the backyard of the mansion. There were many slave dwellings, including four structures organized around a central courtyard, each made of brick. A section of the plantation known as the Field Quarter provided housing for over 50 slaves who worked in Jackson's fields. The Field Quarter buildings were duplexes with limestone foundations, root cellars made of brick, chimneys, one window, and one door that faced the courtyard. Each building was approximately twenty feet wide by twenty feet long, and it was in these small spaces that whole families of slaves lived. At least three areas of the Hermitage property were used for housing slaves. In addition to the original First Hermitage house and the Field Quarter, the north yard of the mansion was also used to provide living quarters to the house slaves. In the north yard one cabin still remains today. Built around 1841, it's referred to as "Alfred's Cabin" because Alfred Jackson lived there as a freedman until he died in 1901. Both sides of the north yard were lined with slave cabins, including two dwellings once located near Alfred's Cabin that have long since disappeared.

On the Hermitage plantation there was a cotton gin house which stored the machinery used to process cotton. Forced human labor was used to grow the cotton demanded by the marketplace, and the cultivation of countless bales of cotton produced the tremendous wealth that Jackson and his family enjoyed. Jackson's fortunes, however, weren't solely tied to this one cash crop. He also formed business partnerships, speculated on land sales, and established businesses such as taverns, horse racing tracks, and a general store. In his busy career he served time in the military, and worked as a lawyer and judge. He was restless; always on the move. When he first started his Hermitage plantation he had just nine slaves. By 1798 the Davidson County Tax Books show that his slaves had increased to fifteen in number. And then the Census of 1820 noted that forty-four belonged to the planter. Jackson also increased the physical size of his domain over the years, aggregating a thousand acres into his plantation, including land for a distillery and a dairy. While two hundred acres were typically farmed in the production of the Hermitage's principal cash crop, cotton, the remaining acreage was dedicated to producing the food needed to support Jackson's family, and his slave population, which approached 150.

On October 13, 1834, the original Hermitage mansion was destroyed in a fire. Jackson's adopted son Andrew, Jr. wrote a letter in an outraged tone to his father in Washington. "The cursed negroes were all so stupid and confused that nothing could be done," he wrote, "until some white one came to their relief" and directed them how to fight the fire. When he learned of the fire, Jackson's own tone remained calm in his written response. "To Andrew Jackson, Jr. Washington, October 23, 1834. Dear Andrew, I have this moment recd. your letter of the 13th instant, giving an account of the unfortunate occurrence of the burning of my dwelling House... The Lord's will be done, it was he that gave me the means to build it, and he has the right to destroy it, and blessed be his name. Tell Sarah cease to mourn its loss. I will have it rebuilt." Jackson quickly hired Joseph Reiff and William Hume, two Nashville architects, and rebuilt the Hermitage mansion in 1835. The repairs were completed in 1836, and this time the mansion stood on the property like a Greek Revival monument.[34]

    The age of Jackson was defined by a small number of white American males seizing the reigns of political power, thoroughly controlling the young republic, and abusing their acquired power by driving Native Americans from their ancestral homelands, and exterminating them if they thought it was necessary, in white America's lust for land and the unquenchable greed fueled by a racist belief in their superiority over non-whites. While Jackson's fortunes flowed forth from his manipulation and control of slave labor, his political career depended more heavily upon the recognition Jackson achieved from his military conquests. Among the military victories was his successful repulsion of British invaders in the War of 1812. And he also became noteworthy for his numerous battles with Native Americans. In 1814 he crushed the Red Sticks, and four years later he captured Bowleg's Town in the first Seminole War. His fame with white Americans grew as he carried forth with the destruction of Native American villages. "I shall penetrate the Creek towns," Jackson declared, "laying waste their villages, burning their houses, killing their warriors and leading into captivity their wives and children until I obtain a surrender." Removal of America's native people was possible because a large majority of white Americans wanted it that way. They had a stake in Jackson's success. His animosity towards non-whites was a culturally inherited value. The founding fathers of the country expressed similar views, including Presidents James Madison and Thomas Jefferson. Madison once wrote, "Next to the case of the black race within our bosom, that of the red man on our borders is the problem most baffling to the policy of our country." And Jefferson, expressing a similarly racist belief in 1803, wrote, "We presume that our strength and their weakness is now so visible, that they must see we have only to shut our hand to crush them." Jackson was following in the legal footsteps of Jefferson and Madison. And in removing Native

Americans from their lands, Jackson argued that he was actually guaranteeing their survival because white Americans would have killed off any Native Americans who remained in their way.[35]

Jackson's destructive efforts in his battles with Native Americans brought him the fame he needed to pursue the highest political position in the land. When elected to the executive office of the United States, he used his power to pass and sign the Indian Removal Bill in May, 1830. It was national legislation written by white politicians and it was designed to speed along the demise of Native Americans wherever they were within the boundaries of the United States. But while he was intent on removing one minority group, he was content to live in close proximity with another minority, the enslaved blacks, so long as that minority group could be continually and thoroughly controlled.

Jackson benefitted from the enslavement of African Americans, and he wanted nothing to do with efforts that threatened to disrupt what he perceived to be the natural order of his world. When the American Anti-Slavery Society began to dispatch thousands of abolitionist pamphlets to the South, the postmaster general decided to stall delivery of the mail, and President Jackson was alerted. Jackson referred to the papers as a "wicked plan of exciting the Negroes to insurrection and to massacre," and in December, 1835, he asked that Congress "prohibit, under severe penalties, the circulation in the southern States, through the mail, of incendiary publications, intended to instigate the slaves to insurrection." The laws of the nation, and of the states that Jackson owned plantations in, already supported the slave owners' legal right to own black people. Now Jackson was asking for the power to abridge the American citizenry's freedom of speech in order to support and defend slavery from the attacks of abolitionists.[36]

Jackson's experience with the enforcement of

slavery extended to the personal level. When his own slaves rebelled and tried to run away from their master, he met their attempts to seek freedom with blunt force. At his Melton Bluff farm three of Jackson's slaves fled from their overseer Egbert Harris. "I have only to say, you know my disposition," Jackson wrote to Harris, "as far as lenity can be extended to these unfortunate creatures, I wish you to do so; subordination must be achieved first, and then good treatment." But when three other slaves escaped from Jackson's plantation in Alabama, Jackson recaptured them all and noted, "although I hate chains, I was compelled to place two of them in irons."[37]

When slaves ran away from Jackson he posted advertisements in the newspapers and offered monetary rewards for their capture. One such slave was Gilbert, who dared to seek his freedom, and Jackson posted this message: "50 Dollar Reward: Ran away from plantation of Gen. Andrew Jackson... in Franklin County... Gilbert, a negro man, about 35 or 40 years of age, very black and fleshy, with a full round face, has a scar on one of his cheeks." Another ad in Nashville's Tennessee Gazette concerning a runaway slave offered a fifty dollar reward for the capture of "a Mulatto Man Slave, about thirty years old, six feet and an inch high, stout made and active, talks sensible, stoops in his walk, and have a remarkable large foot." The ad went on to guarantee reasonable expenses, plus "ten dollars extra, for every hundred lashes any person will give him, to the amount of three hundred." Once slaves ran away, where could they go to remain free? They lived in a land dominated by whites, and one in which the vast majority of black people were slaves. If confronted, they had to account for their freedom. And once away from their master's plantation they had to find some way to acquire the food and shelter needed to survive. Runaway slaves lived in perpetual fear of being apprehended, and for good reason because many of the southern planters had multiple means at their disposal to recapture their human property. The whole environment surrounding plantations served as a substantial barrier to freedom and life outside of slavery.[38]

What little care planters like Jackson occasionally showed towards their human chattel was often a matter of self-interested concern. Jackson once became alarmed at one of his overseer's treatment of his slaves. But his concern for their wellbeing was really due to his desire to maintain his property in good working condition, rather than a genuine concern for the physical and emotional soundness of his slaves. "I have just... recd a letter," Jackson wrote to his son, "advising me of the death of my negroman Jim. I pray you my son to examine minutely into this matter... My negroes shall be treated humanely... Since I have left home I have lost three of my family - Old Ned, I expected to die, but I am fearful the death of Jack, & Jim, has been produced by exposure & bad treatment - your Uncle John Donelson writes, that Steel has ruled with a rod of iron... Unless he changes his conduct, dismiss him." For possibly causing the death of his slaves, Jackson was willing to fire his overseer, but that was all. No further punishment for murder. Simply preventative measures were to be taken so that more of Jackson's human property wouldn't be lost in the future.[39]

Jackson's treatment of his slaves as property is also revealed in the letters he wrote to his wife Rachel. In a letter to her written on October 17, 1814, he expressed a typical planter's interest in the buying and selling of slaves. "Advise me whether the Bills of sale of Sampson & his family & the other negroes Bought has reached you," Jackson wrote.[40]

Little is known about individual slaves who lived at the Hermitage. Two of the slaves that Jackson purchased were born in the early 1790s. One was named Aaron, and the other was Hannah. These two eventually married and had a large family consisting of ten sons and daughters. Hannah became Rachel Jackson's personal assistant and head of the house servants, while Aaron learned and practiced the blacksmith trade.

Another slave family belonging to Jackson was that of Old Hannah, her daughter Betty, and her two sons George and Squire. Old Hannah and Betty served the Jackson family as cooks. George became the family's carriage driver, while his brother Squire ran the cotton press. The brothers also served Jackson as personal assistants. A letter from Jackson to his wife demonstrates how easily these people could be moved around at his command. "Bring squire with such other servants as you may choose," wrote Jackson.[41]

All the personal assistants to Jackson's family, from Aaron and Hannah, to Old Hannah, Betty, Squire, and George, were important pieces to the complex Hermitage puzzle with its broad range of interpersonal and social relationships and hierarchies. The personal assistants who attended to the needs of Jackson's family had access to better food, shelter, and clothing than did those slaves who labored in the cotton fields, and they certainly performed preferable work. But they were no different from the field slaves in at least two important aspects. One, obviously, was that no slaves were free. The other was Jackson's preference for slave families. Family-based slave communities were easier for Jackson and his overseers to control. The discipline meted out against his slaves was reduced, so Jackson thought, because slaves feared being separated from their families. Jackson also recognized that slaves would be less willing to run away if it meant leaving behind family members. The physical barriers of a detention facility with fences and walls didn't need to be present in order to keep Jackson's slaves firmly confined to the plantation grounds. Jackson, and slave planters throughout the United States, eliminated the hope of freedom from their black slaves by the use of psychological barriers linked to family connections. And legal barriers backed by the threat of force and severe punishment contributed to the oppression.

Andrew Jackson purchased his first slave in 1794, and he continued buying slaves throughout his life, with the largest number he owned being roughly 150. When the end of his life drew near he drafted his will, dated June 7, 1843, and in it he gave to his adopted son Andrew, Jr. "the tract of Land whereon I now live known by the Hermitage... with all my negroes, that I may die possessed of... to him and his heirs forever." Unlike George Washington who gave his slaves their freedom in his will, Andrew Jackson gave his slaves to his descendants for all eternity. Among the last words he was said to have spoken to his family as he lay there dying were, "My dear children, and friends, and servants, I hope and trust to meet you all in Heaven, both white and black – both white and black."[42]

Andrew Jackson, Jr. continued to grow cotton at the Hermitage after his father passed away, and dairy products became an increasingly important part of the Hermitage's income. But some bad business decisions and plummeting cotton prices spelled disaster for Jackson's heirs. Andrew Jackson, Jr. fell deeper into debt and the peculiar institution that held humans in bondage at the Hermitage began to fail under his mismanagement.

"Picking, from Scenes on a Cotton Plantation," by A. R. Waud, 1867.

President Andrew Jackson's Hermitage plantation.

five

Stephen Duncan's Natchez

Empowered by Slavery

Chapter 5: Stephen Duncan's Natchez

In the state of Mississippi, in a district known as Natchez, one of the nation's largest slave owners resided in and administered his plantations. Natchez functioned as Mississippi's first capital, and the district stretched from Bayou Sara in the south, to Bayou Pierre in the north, running east along the Mississippi River. Stephen Duncan came to Mississippi from the North, and he brought with him a business manager's mindset, always looking for ways to maximize profits, minimize losses, and secure quality assets at reasonable prices. Duncan was born in 1787 and graduated with a degree in medicine in 1805 when he was still a very young man. Though he was trained to be a doctor, it was Duncan's knowledge of finance and capitalism, combined with the South's agriculture and slavery, that created a hybrid of industrial driven production. Laborers bonded to Duncan by the institution of slavery were forced to produce work for their master in an oppressive system supported by national, state, and local laws. Duncan held thousands of human beings in bondage, and primarily kept his distance from those he enslaved, never recognizing their humanity.

Duncan left the North when he was just a young man to seek his fortunes in what was then considered to be the western limits of the American frontier. He began cotton and sugar plantations in Mississippi, and initially worked alongside the slaves in his fields. Then he married into a rich family and his fortunes continued to rise. He built his Homochito and Walnut Grove slave plantations, and he carried a half interest in a Chapitoulas plantation. In the year 1817 he expressed his desire to build "a sugar house, negro cabins – and the year after – a dwelling house."[43]

By the late 1810s Duncan owned and completely controlled the lives of seventy-three slaves. As his fortunes rose and as the amount of land and number of slaves he owned increased, the amount of time he spent working with his slaves greatly decreased. He began to have much less personal contact with each of the people who labored for him. They were impersonally thought of as property; merely components of a capitalist system that was driven by the goal of obtaining more and more wealth. And when diseases such as small pox killed some of his slaves Duncan was mostly concerned with the impact the epidemics had on his plantation's ability to produce.[44]

The wealthy Butler family that Duncan married into owned a slave plantation with seventy-nine slaves living and working on farmland that was very close to Duncan's own. Slaves from the two plantations established and maintained friendships and relationships beyond the geographical boundaries that they were confined to by law. Additionally, decreased personal contact between slave and master may have afforded the slaves the possibility of greater personal freedoms.

Between 1825 and 1830 Duncan increased his holdings further by purchasing 3,500 acres and seventy-eight more slaves. The money earned by his management of slaves was reinvested in more and more land and slaves. The enterprise became an increasingly impersonal business proposition from the standpoint of the owner. In order to compete with other plantations producing the same type of crops, it was in Duncan's interest to grow, expand, and diversify his holdings, and the bulk of his planting career was spent continuously acquiring more land, equipment, and human property. In 1828 alone Duncan paid sixty-six thousand dollars for vast tracts of land by the Mississippi River, along with sixty-eight slaves whose labor was needed to make the land valuable. The slaves that Duncan selected were part of an overall plan that closely monitored the requirements of his business. The type of laborers, and the number of laborers, had a direct impact on his bottom line.[45]

Duncan's family resided in Auburn, a mansion in

Natchez designed in the grand southern style of the antebellum South. By the end of the 1820s Duncan owned or controlled over forty thousand acres of plantation property upon which three hundred people, owned by Duncan, worked in the fields for his benefit. There were other white families in Mississippi who owned thousands of acres, and hundreds of slaves, and collectively the vast number of slaves became a legitimate concern for the masters. Despite the institution's ability to enforce the slave and master system, Duncan began to worry about large numbers of black people posing a numerical threat to the whites, who were a small minority, and one that was continuing to lose ground demographically. Threats of rebellion and insurrection increased, especially as news spread about slave rebellions in other states. Sometimes it surfaced in the form of maroons · hiding places where slaves fled to escape slavery. From these posts runaway slaves stole food, threatened violence, and assisted other runaways. With fears of a large rebellion in his mind, Duncan did little to combat the maroons. His business sense determined that it was better to accept small losses in the normal operation of his plantations rather than risk a more severe disruption, or the complete collapse of the system.

Nat Turner's Rebellion, a violent episode between slaves and whites in Virginia, led to a growing sense of fear in Duncan's district. Whites tightened their already rigid forms of control over enslaved blacks. "I have great apprehension," said Duncan, "that we will one day have our throats cut in this country." Slave owners like Duncan knew that their ownership of slaves, and their support of the institution of slavery, was inherently wrong. However, the personal financial rewards for maintaining such a system were great enough to take the associated risks and encourage the development of intricate philosophical theories that supported the continuation of the system.[46]

The proportions of enslaved black people to free

whites in some southern regions such as Natchez may have been as high as five to one. "We have here 5 black to one white," wrote Duncan, "and within 4 hours march of Natchez there are 2200 able bodied male slaves." Adams County had eleven thousand blacks living in an area with only four thousand whites. "It is certain our numbers are at present, sufficiently large," wrote Duncan, "to excite serious apprehension for our safety." While Duncan sensed the possibility of danger, he deftly handled problems associated with the management of slaves by avoiding physical punishment, preferring instead to sell uncooperative slaves rather than risk the unknown consequences that might otherwise result. He instructed his managers not to deal too harshly with slaves under their control for fear of them running away, and thereby further taxing plantation resources. Duncan's theory of slave management changed over time. He became a more lenient master in terms of the physical force and corporal punishment typically used to control those he held in bondage.[47]

Stephen Duncan benefitted immensely from the enslavement of hundreds of people and he built great mountains of wealth through the exploitation of their labor, but he was also a forward thinking individual who sensed that the system that was rewarding him so well was an unsustainable system that would eventually collapse. He began to concern himself with questions that made other Southerners uncomfortable. He wanted to know what the future economic life of the South was, and he wanted to know how black and white people were going to live together with or without slavery. He recognized the fact that large numbers of slaves were being imported into the region to support the ever expanding plantation system and that it was bound to reach a point where the black people, so long confined to subservient status and denied basic human rights, would one day rise up against their white oppressors and overthrow those who would keep them enslaved. Duncan wanted to slow the growth of slave populations in Mississippi, but then the Indian Removal Act of 1830 ushered in a new era of expansion as Native Americans were forced from their lands and whites moved in. The Choctaw Indians in particular lost their homelands, and greedy slave owning planters rushed into Mississippi with hundreds and thousands of new slaves to begin working the soil, all in the name of capitalism, expansion, and progress. Duncan's efforts to slow the surging population of blacks living in Mississippi were only halfhearted. On the one hand he argued that the best solution for securing a strong and vibrant future for the state of Mississippi would come through the diversification of its economy and the growth and expansion of different and more complex industries such as textile manufacturing. But on the other hand Duncan's efforts to begin industries of his own were almost always supported by the use of labor supplied by his slaves.[48]

Duncan sensed another threat to the established social order when he realized what could happen when large numbers of slaves were freed by their masters. He believed that overproduction threatened the South because the economic side effects often left plantation owners in a quandary about what they needed to do to survive. Money coming in from the sale of plantation products could dwindle to such an extent, as a result of overproduction, that there wouldn't be enough funds available to continue supporting the slaves working in the system. Planters wouldn't be able to afford food or clothing for their slaves, and in such circumstances they'd be forced to simply release their slaves from bondage, making them free people. And Duncan feared an event of this nature could happen to such a great extent that the entire slave system would collapse.

One plan Duncan supported to spur the growth and diversification of industries in the South included protectionist duties that would provide an edge to the region's enterprises. He also suggested that surplus revenues generated by the new industries could eventually be used to transport large numbers of black slaves out of the country. It would essentially place people of African descent back on to ships destined for Africa as part of his larger plan to phase out slavery completely. According to Duncan, "A century or more would be required for the extinguishment of slavery." And no allowance would be made in these plans for any African Americans to stay and share in the country that they had helped to build.[49]

Duncan's fear led to an attempted realization of his plans to remove former slaves to Africa, and in 1835 the first such cargo of former slaves boarded the Rover, a ship chartered by Duncan that set sail for Liberia. The fact that slaves were being freed by masters in their wills created such a stir, however, that the Mississippi House of Representatives declared that the manumission of slaves through their wills would set a dangerous precedent. It was made illegal in 1841, and Duncan's plans regarding what to do with freed slaves died as well.[50]

In the 1830s, Stephen Duncan's holdings increased to over 18,600 acres and 440 slaves. His business savvy enabled his wealth to increase even during harsh economic downturns. One such economic slump occurred in 1836 prompted in part by Andrew Jackson's Specie Circular Act. The legislation mandated that only gold and silver was acceptable payment for public land. And Henry Clay's Deposit Act of that same year further squeezed funds out of the state of Mississippi, redistributing surplus revenues and putting financial stress on the state. The end result of these two pieces of legislation was that less paper money was issued by the banks, and banks began to call in loans to meet their obligations. Silver and gold were in short supply, and the overall effect was diminished access to funding and a general decline in the economic health of the whole country, with states such as Mississippi being hit particularly hard. The status of Duncan's fortunes, however, was one of increasing wealth, larger land ownership, and a growing number of slaves.

During the 1840s Stephen Duncan acquired over eleven thousand more acres and 275 more slaves. His net worth exceeded two million dollars. He owned over $800,000 in slaves, over $400,000 in land, and $480,000 in stocks and bonds. And he could account for $200,000 in money he loaned out. As one of the wealthiest planters in the region Duncan found himself in the position of frequently serving his community as a lender. His vast reserves of money became an instrument through which he could increase his wealth simply by putting his money to work for him. If the money that Duncan loaned out was paid back on time, then Duncan benefitted when he collected interest on the loan. And if the borrower defaulted on payments owed to Duncan, then he could take ownership of more property. In one instance a promissory note was returned by Duncan in exchange for over one thousand acres of land and sixty-seven slaves.[51]

One recipient of Duncan's loans was Charles Dahlgren, a man who became a Confederate brigadier general during the Civil War. Before the war, Dahlgren was a landowner who had substantial debts to pay, including three notes owed to Duncan. Despite accepting money from Duncan, Dahlgren thought of Duncan as a northerner, and when the time for war drew near, he suspected Duncan would aid the North.[52]

As Duncan's personal wealth increased to ever greater heights he became more interested in redistributing his wealth throughout his family. To his son Henry he gave the Ellisle plantation and over one hundred slaves for Henry's twenty-first birthday. As Duncan spread his wealth out among his family members their plantations increased in number. In the 1840s they owned the Carlisle, Oakley, and Holly Ridge plantations. They also owned L'Argent, Camperdown, Oxford, Duncannon, and others. Each of these plantations had scores of slaves confined to them.

Ownership and management of such vast enterprises in multiple locations came with frequent challenges that threatened Duncan's bottom line. One such challenge came in the form of cholera which spread rapidly through Duncan's slave populations and claimed the lives of 130 slaves. As the health of Duncan's labor force withered and many of his workers died, the crops in his fields did the same since no one was available to care for them. And Duncan seemed to be more concerned with the loss of his harvest than he was with the suffering of his slaves.[53]

In the 1850s Stephen Duncan foresaw the violent troubles that lay ahead and he began to consolidate properties that had accumulated to tens of thousands of acres and thousands of slaves. He sold off large sections of land, and he continued to transfer ownership of other portions to family members such as his son Stephen, Jr. to whom he gave the Carlisle plantation and nearly 150 slaves. However, even with his efforts to consolidate and downsize his holdings, the Federal census records of 1860 show that the total number of his slaves actually increased to over 2200 human beings. The family's combined population of slaves made them one of the largest enslavers of humanity in the South.[54]

The Duncan fortune was amassed by forcing many hundreds of slaves to labor for the benefit of a single family. The power that Stephen Duncan enjoyed in American society was derived from the raw human energy provided by black slavery. Hard labor and disease, sales and transfers, and the physical punishments and violent death associated with the lives of slaves were all part and parcel of the Duncan family's plantation system, yet, despite these oppressive difficulties, slaves managed to carry on underground networks of support that offered strength and comfort to those in desperate need of such sanctuaries.[55]

The highest peak of slave plantation production in the South was reached just prior to the commencement of the American Civil War. More slaves worked on more acreage and produced more commodities than ever before. The Duncan plantations were producing hogsheads of sugar by the thousands, and thousands of bales of cotton. They were also producing tens of thousands of gallons of molasses, and tens of thousands of bushels of corn, all for the enrichment of a small number of whites related to one man - Stephen Duncan.

Duncan benefitted tremendously from his strong connections to northern markets. The last thing he wanted was for the South to secede from the Union. A New York Times article from December, 1860, reported that Duncan said the slavery question shouldn't be brought before Congress again so that America could remain "a united and happy people, with all these vexatious, ruinous, and embarrassing questions settled, possessing a government and a Union, beyond all comparison the best on earth." But in response to the rapidly shifting political conditions, Duncan transferred his business interests to the North, moved there himself in 1863, and invested in U.S. bonds during the war. The war brought to an end the system of slavery that made him so wealthy, but he still remained tremendously rich.[56]

As an absentee planter, Duncan rarely met the people that he had enslaved. Face to face contact with these people who labored for him in his fields seldom occurred, and the concept of planter paternalism never interested him. To large plantation owners such as Duncan, slaves weren't considered to be human. There was no discussion about their equality, and no empathy for their condition. On paper Duncan owned a million dollars worth of human beings, but he never took the time to write about anything personal concerning his slaves. He never discouraged slaves from getting married, and simply considered such relationships to be effective methods of keeping slaves from running away or rebelling. But as a slave master Duncan had the power to end such relationships at any moment. With a simple directive, one of his human assets could be sold away in a cold, industrial manner. A husband and wife could forever be separated by a sale that solely benefitted their master, and the institution of marriage could be trumped by the institution of slavery.

Stephen Duncan, Natchez, Mississippi.

Stephen Duncan's "Auburn" plantation home.

Empowered by Slavery

six

Jefferson Davis'
Brierfield

Empowered by Slavery

Chapter 6: Jefferson Davis' Brierfield

The president of the Southern Confederacy, Jefferson Davis, was the tenth and last child of his parents. He was born in Kentucky in 1808, and his family moved to Mississippi in 1810. He grew up in Woodville and Poplar Grove, attended Catholic school, and then went to military school. Davis' father died when he was just sixteen years old and his brother Joseph assumed a paternal role in his life, encouraging the young man to go to West Point. President Andrew Jackson became a hero and an idol to Jefferson Davis. "He inspired reverence and affection that has remained with me through my whole life," said Davis. Like Jackson, Davis served his country in the United States military. And like Jackson, Davis eventually owned slaves and operated a large plantation.[57]

In 1835 Davis resigned his commission in order to become a cotton planter. He married his first wife, Sarah Knox Taylor, the daughter of Zachary Taylor · the 12th President of the United States and a slave owner himself. Together, Jefferson and Sarah were about to begin what they thought would be a long life of living and working on a Mississippi plantation when Sarah became ill and died, possibly of malaria. They had been married for only three months.

Davis' brother Joseph gave a portion of his Davis Bend farms to Jefferson Davis, and it became the plantation known as Brierfield, a name stemming from the dense growth of briers flourishing upon the land. Then his brother took him to Natchez, Mississippi, where they purchased ten black slaves for Davis' use. Having suffered the tragic loss of his wife, Davis threw himself into clearing and planting his farmlands where he worked long hard hours alongside his slaves.

Among the first of Davis' slaves was a man named James Pemberton. Though neither man knew it at the time, it was the beginning of a long relationship in which both men came to deeply respect the other, and Davis trusted Pemberton perhaps more than even his own brother. Pemberton became Davis' overseer at the Brierfield plantation, and he proved his worth to Davis one year when he managed the production of 170,000 pounds of cotton.

Ten years after the death of his first wife, Davis married Varina Banks Howell, a merchant's daughter in Natchez. She was the woman who shared with Davis the best and worst moments of life, including the birth of their children, and the collapse of the South with the defeat of the Confederacy. Together they lived and worked at the Brierfield plantation, a farmland encompassing over eight hundred acres. It included over seventy slaves by the time of their marriage. In the late 1840s work on the Brierfield mansion was completed, and life for the Davis family was good. But then tragedy struck in 1850 when Pemberton died of pneumonia.

With Pemberton's help, the Brierfield plantation became a productive farm, and Davis became a benign slave owner. Davis allowed his slaves to name themselves, rather than practicing the planter tradition of choosing nicknames for them. On the Davis plantation there was no use of corporal punishment, and when a slave was accused of something, Davis insisted on asking the accused slave their side of the story, saying, "I will ask him to give me his account of it." He also believed in being kind to his slaves, remarking, "I cannot allow any negro to outdo me in courtesy." Years later, a woman named Florida, who had once been a slave on the Brierfield plantation, said, "We had good grub and good clothes and nobody worked hard. Dem Davis's never would let nobody touch one of their niggers."[58]

Though a busy planter, Davis was also an active politician. He served in the United States Senate, and as secretary of war. During his time in Washington, Varina spent many days without her husband back at their plantation. She was kept busy making clothes for the slaves, or caring for them when they were ill. At Brierfield she tried to maintain the standards her husband had set, but unlike her husband she had no objection to selling slaves and splitting families apart.

While in Washington, Davis had opportunities to interact with people from different regions throughout the United States, and these included abolitionists from the North. In the Senate, Davis argued that slaves were better off in slavery than they would be as free people. He said that black people benefitted from their close "association with a more elevated race." And when abolitionists predicted violent uprisings by the slaves, he responded by saying, "Our doors are unlocked at night... We lie down to sleep trusting to them for our defence, and the bond between the master and the slave is as near as that which exists between capital and labor anywhere."[59]

Though full of racist and prejudicial overtones, much of what Davis said regarding slavery was true, as he saw it. He had successfully created a relatively peaceful environment upon his plantation, and years later former slaves expressed similar sentiments regarding Davis' treatment of the black people confined to his farms. One former slave was William Samford who said, "That I loved him this shows, and I can say that every colored man whom he ever owned loved him. He was a good, kind master." Perhaps part of the slaves' respect for Davis came from their recognition of their condition, trapped in a state of perpetual servitude in which the world beyond the boundaries of their own plantation acted in concert to restrict the mobility and livelihoods of slaves, and the environment created in such a world offered too many opportunities for the ruthless exploitations that all too frequently accompanied the master and slave relationship. Upon the lands of other plantations cruel overseers might whip their slaves until blood poured from their bodies. At the Brierfield plantation, slaves were allowed to own chickens, and plant gardens, and have some measure of control over their lives. Davis' work camp was an oasis within a sea of trouble.[60]

Davis cherished the lifestyle he and his brother Joseph had created at Davis Bend. And they both enjoyed the advantages afforded to wealthy white people that the southern economic system had to offer. Jefferson Davis liked the deference shown to him by his black slaves, and his temperament and personality were such that he believed white people should pay him the same form of respect. But white people did not, because they saw themselves as being Davis' equal. However, white people did believe in Davis enough to vote for him, and they elected him to serve in public offices. Once installed in office, he argued for the southern cause, and he fought political battles that supported the existence, continuance, and expansion of the institution of slavery within the boundaries of the United States. He cited the Bible as the "authority for the establishment of slavery among men, and... the Constitution for its recognition throughout the United States." And when his slave-owning hero Andrew Jackson died in 1845, Davis said, "My affection and admiration followed him to his grave, and cling to his memory."[61]

Like Davis, Andrew Jackson had purchased more and more slaves throughout his life and accumulated a grand fortune through his exploitation of black people. And like Davis, Andrew Jackson had enjoyed a successful military career. But Andrew Jackson rose to the presidency of the United States, and believed in a strong federal government, while Jefferson Davis became the president of the Confederacy and supported the belief that the states had the right to secede from the union. Their personal histories produced wildly different outcomes for the two men who had lived similar lives. The younger of the two idolized the other and wanted to mirror his hero in so many ways. But the revolution of the wheel of fortune that

Thomas Jefferson once spoke of slid out from beneath the feet of Jefferson Davis and it meant the destruction of his status in American society.

In February 1861, the seceded states elected Jefferson Davis to be president of the Confederacy. The Confederate Constitution guaranteed the right of white people to own black slaves and it stated that no law shall be made that will deny or impair "the right of property in negro slaves." When the Civil War started southern planters like Davis dreamt of extending slavery west towards the Pacific Ocean, and south toward Central America. But by 1862, the Union Army was already making progress towards reclaiming territory from the seceded states. In June of that year the Brierfield plantation was sacked by the Union Army, and Joseph Davis' Hurricane plantation was torched by the soldiers. Davis Bend was confiscated by the federal government. Union soldiers cut up carpet in Davis' mansion and used pieces for saddle blankets. They tore down drapes and used them for tents. And Davis' papers and books were torn up, scattered, burned, and carried away. Personal letters were taken and published in the newspapers. At the war's half way point Jefferson Davis had already lost his home, and his slaves were free of his control. But from Richmond, Davis continued on with his leadership of the southern cause. "The Northern portion of Virginia has been ruthlessly desolated," Jefferson Davis mourned, "the people not only deprived of the means of subsistence, but their household property destroyed, and every indignity which the base imagination of a merciless foe could suggest inflicted!" Unfortunately for Davis, he could speak of these things from the vantage point of personal experience.[62]

In April of 1863 Joseph Davis wrote to his younger brother and noted the difficult nature of maintaining control over personal property when the countryside all around them was ravaged by war. "I can say but little favorable of our farming interests," Joseph wrote. In June of that same year Joseph explained, "As regards the negroes the promises made them were more than they could resist, how much force was used I do not know, but their departure was sudden & in the night, The negroes saw the country in the power of the enemy and believed that their orders must be obeyed." But during the course of the Union Army's stay at Davis Bend, one slave, Hagar, who was questioned by the soldiers, said that Jefferson Davis was a good master and that she didn't want to leave. And in a letter written to Davis by Jefferson Bradford the author stated that the slaves "loved you and would do just what you wanted them to do."[63]

In September of 1941, the former slave George Johnson was interviewed about his experience living on a plantation and working for Jefferson Davis. "I got my name from President Jeff Davis," said Johnson. "He was president of the Southern Confederacy. He owned my grandfather and my father. Brought them from Richmond, Virginia... Everyone learned tend to master Jeff's business. Everyone admired him. Obeyed him... They would always obey him all the time. White and black." Johnson went on to say that Davis didn't allow anything to happen to his slaves, and he made sure that they were treated right. "When he wanted things done he just put it on paper and it's gone. It done. He had no trouble at all. All his niggas had a common education. All of them."[64]

Though historical accounts of some Brierfield slaves portrayed Davis in a good light, the black people on the plantation were living in a state of human bondage. Slaves at Davis Bend worked long and hard, sometimes even into the darkest hours of night, picking all of the cotton that made Davis rich. While his white family enjoyed the wealth of plantation life, living in a one-story mansion complete with a library, study, multiple bedrooms, a dining room, a huge back porch, and marble mantles imported from Italy for the parlor, Davis's slaves in contrast lived a life of abject poverty in humble single room quarters, and children of these slaves were said to have eaten their breakfast meals from a trough. When the Union Army came to Davis Bend, Brierfield ceased to function as a camp of concentrated, enslaved labor.

"Am I not a Man and a Brother?" Published 1837. Library of Congress, copy-free, public domain.

"Five Generations on Smith's Plantation, Beaufort, South Carolina," by T. H. O'Sullivan, 1862. Library of Congress, copy-free, public domain.

Empowered by Slavery

seven

Robert E. Lee's Arlington

Empowered by Slavery

Chapter 7: Robert E. Lee's Arlington

Robert E. Lee, the highest ranking military officer in the Confederacy, lived on a plantation known as Arlington, and he owned dozens of slaves prior to the Civil War. Members of Robert Lee's family were descendants of Richard Lee, an immigrant to the Virginia colony in 1641. Robert was the youngest son of Henry Lee, a governor of Virginia who had once served as a lieutenant under George Washington. The Lees became of one the richest plantation owning families in Virginia. But Henry Lee made poor decisions that stripped the family of much of its wealth, and Robert, as the youngest son of Henry, was left with a comparatively small inheritance.

Robert Lee, however, was a friend of the Custis family, wealthy slave owners that possessed four large tracts of farmland, with one of those plantations being Arlington in Virginia. Robert had an established career in the military when he married into the Custis family by taking Mary Custis as his wife. As Robert continued to serve his country by accepting military assignments that took him far from home, Mary stayed behind at their home in Arlington. Even though he was often away on duty, Robert Lee was once again a part of a wealthy, slave owning plantation family.

Mary Custis Lee's father was George Washington Custis, a grandson of Martha Washington. At the time of Robert Lee's marriage to Mary, George Custis was the legal owner of Arlington and its sixty human slaves, many of whom George inherited from Martha Washington when she passed away. George became one of the largest holders of slaves in the state with nearly two hundred, including those who lived and worked at the Romancoke and White House plantations.

In 1802 the first Custis slaves began to inhabit Arlington, and they constructed their own cabin housing with logs taken from the plantation's forest, and bricks made of the farm's red clay soil. The slave quarters were simple rectangular shapes with two or three rooms and a stone floor. When not erecting structures, slaves were put to work clearing the fields and planting and harvesting the corn and wheat that was produced for market.

Similar to the slave plantations of Thomas Jefferson and James Madison, Arlington was an estate that went under long periods of construction. George Custis fashioned himself a mansion in a Grecian style with tall white columns and an eighteen foot ceiling. While the center section was constructed in 1818, a final parlor section was added decades later in 1850 under the guidance of Robert Lee. The Custis family had a grand home to live in that dominated the estate with its physical size, leaving the much smaller slave quarters and other outbuildings dwarfed in comparison.

George Washington Custis inherited most of his wealth, and was thus born a rich planter, but he apparently had little of the interest required to grow and expand the family business. "Negro property is of great and increasing value," George Custis said, but "I have no desire to add one more." He didn't like the responsibility of directly managing his human chattel, so he left the supervision to overseers who were almost always temporary components of the slave plantation system at Arlington, and their frequent turnover, combined with lackluster supervision, left the estate in a precarious condition, suffering from poor maintenance and an increasing pile of debt. Among the directions given to his overseers was George Custis' instruction to keep the slaves "well fed, well clothed, treated fairly & kept in proper subjugation to those who are placed over them." The strange condition in which slaves found themselves at Arlington was one in which they existed in a relatively benign environment, yet one that still expected "subjugation" of the slaves to the master. However, George

Custis' relationship with slavery changed over time, and he actually became interested in the possibility of transporting black slaves back to Africa. Like James Madison, Custis joined the American Colonization Society in 1817, though the effort failed.[65]

George Custis had married Molly Fitzhugh in 1804, a woman who disliked slavery, and who encouraged her husband to free his slaves in his will and thereby end his family's connection with the evil institution. When George Custis died in 1857, Mary Lee inherited Arlington. But the wording of George Custis' will concerning the freedom of his slaves launched one of the more complex legal battles that Robert Lee confronted in his lifetime. It was a strange struggle in the courts that lasted well into the course of the American Civil War. Though George Custis' will had apparently allowed for his slaves to become free people, Robert Lee was prepared to fight it in court.

One of the Custis family's slaves was Wesley Norris whose story was published by the National Slavery Standard, an antislavery newspaper, in 1866. "My name is Wesley Norris; I was born a slave on the plantation of George Park Custis," said Norris. "After the death of Mr. Custis, Gen. Lee, who had been made executor of the estate, assumed control of the slaves, in number about seventy; it was the general impression among the slaves of Mr. Custis that on his death they should be forever free; in fact this statement had been made to them by Mr. C. years before; at his death we were informed by Gen. Lee that by the conditions of the will we must remain slaves for five years." Robert Lee didn't free the Custis slaves when his father-in-law died, and he did everything he could to hold them in bondage for at least the five year period he thought his family was entitled to. Norris continued, "I remained with Gen. Lee about seventeen months, when my sister Mary, a cousin of ours, and I determined to run away, which we did in the year 1859; we had already reached Westminster, in Maryland, on our way to the North, when we were apprehended and thrown into prison fifteen days, when we were sent back to Arlington; we were immediately taken before Gen. Lee, who demanded the reason why we ran away; we frankly told him that we considered ourselves free; he then told us he would teach us a lesson we never would forget; he then ordered us to the barn, where in his presence, we were tied firmly to posts by a Mr. Gwin, our overseer, who was ordered by Gen. Lee to strip us to the waist and give us fifty lashes each, excepting my sister, who received but twenty; we were accordingly stripped to the skin by the overseer, who, however, had sufficient humanity to decline whipping us; accordingly Dick Williams, a county constable was called in, who gave us the number of lashes ordered; Gen Lee in the meantime, stood by, and frequently enjoined Williams to 'lay it on well,' an injunction which he did not fail to heed; not satisfied with simply lacerating our naked flesh, Gen. Lee then ordered the overseer to thoroughly wash our backs with brine, which was done." This account from Norris was echoed by similar newspaper accounts that reported the Custis slaves were legally freedmen, and illegally held by Lee.[66]

An anonymous letter to the editor of the New York Tribune, published in June of 1859, suggested that the author of the letter witnessed the barbarism of slavery at Arlington. "I live one mile from the plantation of George Washington P. Custis, now Col. Lee's, as Custis willed it to Lee. All the slaves on this estate, as I understand, were set free at the death of Custis," wrote the author, "but are now held in bondage by Lee... Last week three of the slaves ran away; an officer was sent after them, overtook them nine miles this side of Pennsylvania, and brought them back. Col. Lee ordered them whipped. They were two men and one woman. The officer whipped the two men, and said he would not whip the woman, and Col. Lee stripped her and whipped her himself... After being whipped, he sent them to Richmond and hired them out as good farm hands."[67]

Slave plantation owners like Robert Lee became delusional in their thoughts concerning the institution of slavery, arguing that the human bondage of black people was good for them, and that the Christian values they were exposed to in America would civilize them and be an uplifting influence in the progress of black people towards a higher level of culture. Slave owners suggested that slavery was just a temporary stepping stone for black people, and they believed that plantation owners were fulfilling God's will, a form of self-justification for the wrongs they were committing. And though the planters argued that they were helping to uplift black people, they were responsible for passing legislation in the state of Virginia that made attempts to educate black people forbidden by law. In 1849 the Virginia House of Delegates made "every assemblage of Negroes for the purpose of instruction in reading or writing... an unlawful assembly." Whites who broke the law by helping blacks to learn could've been sentenced to six months in jail. Plantation owners argued that slavery was beneficial to both black and white people. But the authority, power, and wealth that the white slave owners enjoyed was built upon a foundation riddled with lies.[68]

The black men and women who lived and worked at the Arlington slave plantation knew that life was not meant to be lived amidst such drudgery and despair. Freedom, and the desire for a better life, prompted many of Arlington's slaves to flee from their imprisonment, and in doing so they frustrated Lee's attempts to turn the fortunes of the plantation around and make the farms profitable again. In 1856 Lee wrote a letter to a Mr. A. Keese in which he asked for help in capturing runaway slaves. "There are two women belonging to the Estate of G. W. P. Custis, now in Washington, where they have been since 1 Jany last," wrote Lee. "One, black, about 35 years old, named Caroline Bingham with a child... has been seen frequently in the centre market, going & returning by N.

7th st. The other, mulatto, about 23 years old, named Catharine Burke, with a nearly white child... has also been seen in the centre market. Last Saturday evening she was seen in Mr. Bryans Grocers store near 7th St. with Austin Syphax, a freedman from this place. They report themselves at service with my consent – I have offered $10 for the apprehension of each of these women, upon their delivery." Lee's letter also reported missing articles that he believed were stolen and listed other slaves by name who had run away.[69]

Lee was in a perpetual state of anger related to the rebellious nature of the Arlington slaves. In 1858 he wrote, "I have had some trouble with some of the people... Reuben, Parks & Edward, in the beginning of the previous week, rebelled against my authority – refused to obey my orders, & said that they were as free as I was, etc., etc. – I succeeded in capturing them however, tied them and lodged them in jail. They resisted until overpowered & called upon the other people to rescue them." For their resistance, Lee placed them in jail for two months, and then hired them out.[70]

Lee's military training and expectation of obedience to his authority clashed with the conditions he found upon assuming a more substantial role in the management of his father-in-law's plantation estate. George Custis had allowed slaves to marry, and to remain with their families. By contrast, Lee wouldn't hesitate to break families apart. Everywhere that Lee looked he found what he considered to be unproductive and inefficient conditions at the Arlington plantation resulting from lackluster management and passive resistance on the part of the slaves. It was "almost useless to attempt improvement," Lee complained, "or to resist the current that has been so long setting against industry & advancement." He was angered at what he perceived to be the laziness inherent in Arlington. When he sought the services of a new overseer to help manage the plantation Lee demanded that the overseer be "an energetic honest farmer, who while he will be considerate & kind to the Negroes, will be firm & make them do their duty." When he ordered a couple of female slaves to pack his clothes he noticed that his new pair of pants disappeared. "They are only one more item to the number that have disappeared," Lee lamented, "perhaps taken off by Spirits, I know not where." Lee came to hate slavery not for the moral dilemma all who were engaged in it faced, but for what he considered to be the terrible responsibility placed on the slave owners who had to make the plantation system somehow work amidst great inefficiencies, and who felt it a tremendous burden to support the life of a slave from birth to death.[71]

Among the slaves born at Arlington was Jim Parks, also known as "Uncle Jim." Born in 1843, Parks could recall the passing of George Custis and his wife in the 1850s. In the 1860s, when the Union took possession of Arlington, Parks assisted with the digging of graves for Civil War soldiers who had fallen during the battles. Years later he recalled that "coffins had been piled in long rows like cordwood" on the Arlington estate, and he could point to where the old slave quarters and cemeteries were, along with the wells, the icehouse, and the blacksmith shop.

Two other slaves on the Arlington plantation were Selina Norris and Thornton Gray, a married couple with eight children. Their entire family lived in a single room in the South Slave Quarters on the Custis estate. Selina was the personal assistant of Mrs. Lee, and it was with Selina that Mrs. Lee entrusted the Arlington keys when the Custis family fled in advance of the oncoming Union Army. When soldiers began to rifle through the Arlington property, it was Selina who rescued artifacts that were connected to George Washington from would-be thieves.

When George Custis died in 1857, Selina, Thornton, Jim Parks, and well over one hundred slaves at the Romancoke, White House, and Arlington plantations were freed in the Custis will. But owing to a technicality,

Robert Lee was able to hold most of them in bondage for an extended period of time that lasted well into the course of the Civil War. Prior to the war, Lee expressed the typical slave plantation owner attitude regarding the controversial nature of slavery when he wrote, "How long their subjugation may be necessary is known & ordered by a wise and Merciful Providence. Their emancipation will sooner result from the mild & melting influence of Christianity, than the storms and tempests of fiery Controversy." Lee's noting the possibility of "storms and tempests" foretold the coming of a terrible conflict. Prior to the Civil War, in 1856, Lee criticized northerners and argued that "these people must be aware that their object is both unlawful and foreign to them and to their duty, and that this institution, for which they are irresponsible and non-accountable, can only be changed by them through the agency of a civil and servile war." As a slave owning planter, Lee felt the pressure leveled against the system that supported his family's way of life, and he was prepared to fight. When the Civil War started, and when Virginia seceded, and when Lee assumed command of the Confederate Army, the struggle for the South to free itself from the North and maintain its peculiar institution commenced.[72]

Despite the state of Virginia's secession from the United States, the state's Court of Appeals still held to the principles of respecting the wills of slave owning planters, and during the Civil War the court decided that the Custis slaves were to be given their freedom. In a letter written by Robert Lee to his wife in January of 1862 Lee wrote, "I have received the decree of the Court of Appeals in reference to your father's will. It has decided all the points. The people are to be emancipated at the end of the five years... The enemy are in possession of Smith's Island & what I am to do with the negroes I do not know." To his son in November of that same year he wrote, "I hope you will be able to arrange for the people whom I wish to liberate the 31 December... Indeed I should like to include the whole list at Arlington." By 1861 the Lee and Custis family had already fled Arlington, which the Union Army took possession of. At the end of 1862 Lee wrote again to his wife: "As regards the servants, those that are hired out can soon be settled. They can be furnished with their free papers... Those that are on the farms I will issue free papers to as soon as I can... I desire to do what is right and best for the people... I wish to close the whole affair, but whether I can do so during the course of the war I cannot say, nor do I know that I shall live to see the end of it." Lee held on to his slaves until the last possible moment, finally allowing them to go free on January 1, 1863, the same day that the Emancipation Proclamation assumed full force.[73]

In an interview conducted by Herbert Saunders after the war, Saunders said that Lee "assured me that he had always been in favour of the emancipation of the negroes, and that in Virginia the feeling had been strongly inclining in the same direction, till the ill-judged enthusiasm (amounting to rancor) of the abolitionists in the North had turned the Southern tide of feeling in the other direction." Southern apologists tried to whitewash the sins of slavery and the war from their heroes, and they pinned the blame for the massive destruction and losses on northern abolitionists. Robert Lee's son, Robert Lee Junior, tried to explain his father's involvement with slavery. He said, "wherein it was directed that all the slaves belonging to the estate should be set free after the expiration of so many years... He proceeded according to the law of the land to carry out the provisions of the will, and had delivered to every one of the servants, where it was possible, their manumission papers."[74]

In the middle of the Civil War, part of Lee's Arlington property became "The Freedmen's Village" in 1863, when the Union Army set up the site as a temporary refuge for former slaves. Abolitionists and northern newspapers reveled in the idea that the Confederate general's estate should be transformed from a place of human bondage into a community of free black people. The Washington DC Morning Chronicle noted, "a happy thought has occurred to the Secretary of War which it gives us great pleasure to record... He ordered Col. Green to organize the Freedmen's Village... upon the Arlington estate." The village took on a life of its own, far exceeding its original purpose, with homes being built and schools opening that offered to train African Americans as shoemakers, carpenters, and blacksmiths. The number of freed black people who called it home surged up to two thousand, and they lived in rows of housing at the southern end of the property located a half mile from the Arlington mansion. The village had a kitchen, a laundry, a schoolhouse, and a home for elderly African Americans.[75]

Slavery at Arlington was legally supported before the Civil War, and the institution recognized fully the rights of Arlington's slave owners to control, manipulate, sell and buy human property, and to enforce their will by way of corporal punishment on offending slaves. The institution's impact on the lives of slaves was heavily influenced by the personality and temperament of the person in charge of the plantation - the one person who had the authority to make life-altering decisions. Under the ownership of George Custis, Arlington slaves enjoyed the benefits of a comparatively benign management system. When authority shifted to Robert Lee in the 1850s, the lives of the Arlington slaves were altered by a man who wasn't afraid to use physical punishment against his human property, and who had no qualms about selling slaves away and splitting families apart. The same human slaves, the same space, the same institution, and the same legal structure, could be dramatically transformed by a single individual. Fortunately, the Union Army, during the course of the Civil War, transformed once again the meaning of what Arlington was. The plantation, once a confining and concentrated space from which black people rarely escaped, became a final resting place for the soldiers who died fighting to preserve the Union. And their sacrifice guaranteed that all Americans were to be free.

A continuity is present in the story of slaves owned by early American leaders. Washington, Jefferson, and Madison were part of America's founding generation, and each man owned slaves before, during, and after their ascension to the highest office in the land. President Andrew Jackson was of a later generation, and followed squarely in the footsteps of his predecessors with his ownership and exploitation of human slaves. American industrial leaders, such as Stephen Duncan of Natchez, sought to capitalize on the freedoms they enjoyed by enslaving many hundreds of people. And southern political and military leaders, such as Jefferson Davis and Robert Lee, risked everything they had by rebelling against their country in an effort to maintain the economic system that benefitted them so well – an economy dominated by the slave plantation system.

Race-based discrimination confined African Americans to plantations. There were many hundreds of these locations throughout the republic. Laws were written to protect the interests of wealthy property owners, and this included legislation that guaranteed the rights of slave owners to do as they pleased with the people they owned. African slaves were tied to specific places. They weren't free to leave, except upon the orders or authorization of their master. If they chose to risk running away, then there was no safe place for them to permanently escape to. The threat of being recaptured always existed. And those who were recaptured often met with grizzly punishments inflicted upon them by their masters.

Robert E. Lee's Arlington plantation, photograph 1861.

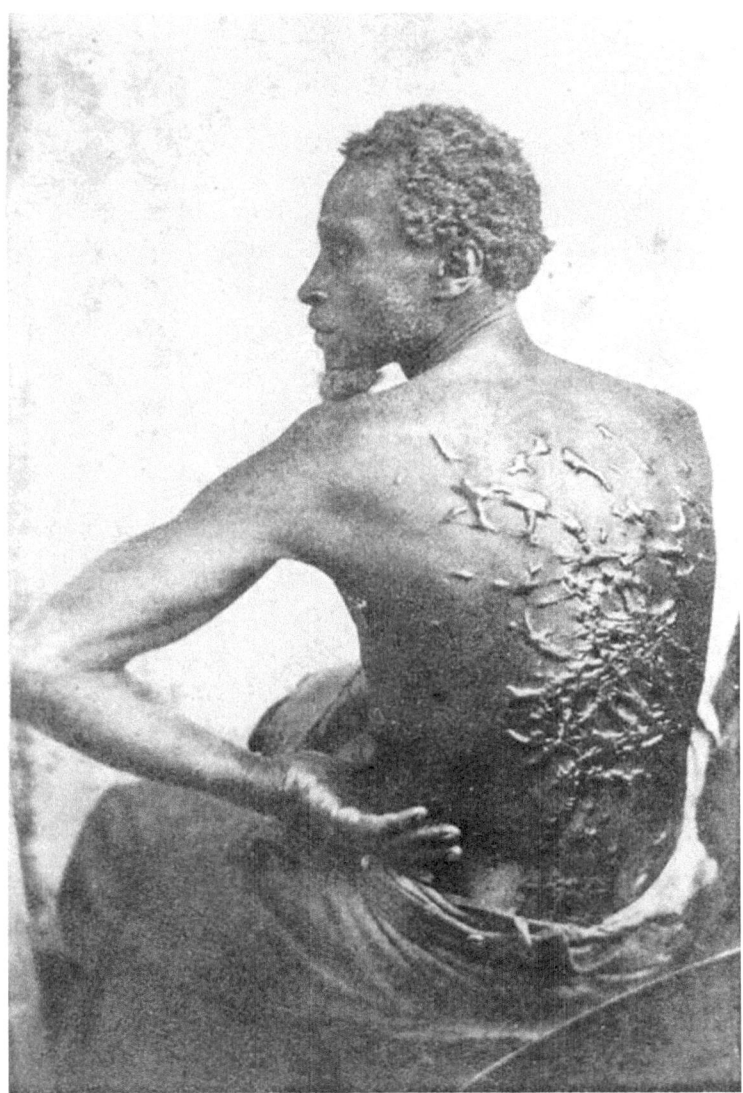

"Peter," by Matthew Brady, 1863.

Empowered by Slavery

.

Conclusion

George Washington, America's first President, and heroic leader of the war for American independence, fought bravely to secure his freedom and the liberty of his countrymen, but he never relinquished his right to personally own slaves. However, he did recognize slavery as being one of the most significant threats to the life of the new nation and said, "Nothing but the rooting out of slavery can perpetuate the existence of our union, by consolidating it in a common bond of principle."

The ghosts of the Civil War still haunt the halls of nineteenth century American history. The crack of the whip, the clanging of the chains, the psychological and physical abuse, and all the other horrid hallmarks of slavery will forever be remembered as emblematic of the era's awful darkness. The young American nation of the 1800s groaned and strained mightily under the weight of a terrible hypocrisy, an inhumane system, and the unjust domination and persecution of the innocent. "I have heard their groans and sighs, and seen their tears," remarked Harriet Tubman of the people she saw enslaved, "and I would give every drop of blood in my veins to free them." Many did in fact do just that, giving all they had in America's Civil War.

Democracy is just like every other human invention. Its machinery needs maintenance and care. The parts must be lubricated, mended, or replaced, as they are subjected to the strains and tribulations of human social intercourse, becoming worn out over time. At this point in history democracy still stands as the truest and greatest friend of freedom and liberty. It's the strongest and surest defense against those who would be tyrants, autocrats, dictators, kings, and aspirants to imperial thrones. Even as America enters into the third millennia, the lies and deceits perpetrated by the few in their megalomaniacal pursuit of power over the many must be treated as no less than acts of treason against humanity. Even in the United States the citizens of the nation must always be on guard against those who would betray the democratic values of shared power, elected government, freedom of speech and religion, and equal protection under the law. There is no difference between slave owner and autocratic tyrant. They're the same devil. The same beast. "The limits of tyrants are prescribed by the endurance of those whom they oppress," Frederick Douglas once said, and "There is not a man beneath the canopy of Heaven who does not know that slavery is wrong for him."

Empowered by Slavery

For Additional Reading

Other books by Adam Platts include *American Internment: World War II Japanese American Internment Camps*. Now available at: Amazon, Barnes and Nobel, Lulu, and Wal-Mart.

Empowered by Slavery

Bibliography

Allen, Felicity. Jefferson Davis: Unconquerable Heart. Columbia: University of Missouri Press, 1999.

Bassett, John Spencer. Correspondence of Andrew Jackson. Washington D.C.: Carnegie Institution of Washington, 1931.

Bernstein, Richard B. Thomas Jefferson. New York: Oxford University Press, 2005.

Betts, Edwin Morris. Thomas Jefferson's Farm Book. Redmond, VA: Thomas Jefferson Memorial Foundation, 1999.

Blassingame, John W. Slave Testimony: Two Centuries of Letters, Speeches, Interviews, and Autobiographies. Louisiana State University, 2003.

Brazy, Martha Jane. An American Planter: Stephen Duncan of Antebellum Natchez and New York. Baton Rouge: Louisiana State University Press, 2006.

Cairnes, John Elliott. The Slave Power: Its Character, Career, & Probable Designs. Bedford, MA: Applewood Books, 1862.

Cooper, William J. Jefferson Davis: The Essential Writings. Random House, Inc. 2004.

Crist, Lynda L. The Papers of Jefferson Davis: Volume 9, January-September 1863. Baton Rouge: LSU Press, 1997.

Davis, Varina. Jefferson Davis: Ex-President of the Confederate States of America – A Memoir by His Wife, Vol. I. New York: Belford Company Publishing, 1890.

Davis, William. Jefferson Davis: The Man and His Hour.
New York: Harper Collins Publishers, 1991.

Dowdey, Clifford. The Wartime Papers of R. E. Lee.
Boston: Little, Brown and Company, 1961.

Dudley, William. American Slavery. San Diego:
Greenhaven Press, Inc., 2000.

Elliot, Jonathan. Debates on the Adoption of the Federal
Constitution, Reported by James Madison. Philadelphia:
J.B. Lippincott & Company, 1876.

Feller, Daniel. Moser, Harold. Moss, Laura-Eve. Coens,
Thomas. The Papers of Andrew Jackson, Volume 7; Volume
1829. Knoxville: University of Tennessee Press, 2007.

Ferling, John E. The First of Men: A Life of George
Washington. Knoxville: University of Tennessee Press,
1988.

Foley, John P. The Jeffersonian Cyclopedia: A
Comprehensive Collection of the Views of Thomas
Jefferson. New York: Funk & Wagnalls Company, 1900.

Gower, Herschel. Charles Dahlgren of Natchez.
Washington D.C.: Brassey's Inc., 2002.

Hattaway, Herman. Jefferson Davis, Confederate
President. Lawrence, KS: University Press of Kansas,
2002.

Hillard, George Stillman. Life, Letters, and Journals of
George Ticknor, Vol. 1. London: Sampson, Low, Marston,
Searle, & Rivington, 1876.

Hirschfeld, Fritz. George Washington and Slavery: A Documentary Portrayal. Columbia: University of Missouri, Columbia, 1997.

James, Marquis. The Life of Andrew Jackson. New York: Garden City Publishing Company, 1940.

James, Marquis. Andrew Jackson: Portrait of a President. New York: Grosset & Dunlap Publishers, 1937.

Jefferson, Thomas. Notes on the State of Virginia. Richmond, VA: Harvard College Library, 1853.

Jennings, Paul. A Colored Man's Reminiscences of James Madison. Brooklyn: G.C.Beadle, 1865.

Ketcham, Ralph Louis. James Madison: A Biography. New York: University of Virginia, MacMillan, 1971.

Lee, Robert E., Jr. Recollections and Letters of General Robert E. Lee. New York: Garden City Publishing Co., Inc., 1924.

Lodge, Henry Cabot. George Washington, Volume 2. Middlesex: The Echo Library.

Long, A. L. Robert E. Lee: His Military and Personal History. Secaucus, NJ: The Blue and Grey Press, 1983.

Marrin, Albert. George Washington and the Founding of a Nation. Dutton Children's Books, 2003.

McLaughlin, Jack. Jefferson and Monticello: The Biography of a Builder. New York: Henry Holt and Company, 1990.

Meacham, Jon. American Lion: Andrew Jackson in the White House. New York: Random House, 2008.

Moore, Virginia. The Madisons: A Biography. San Francisco: McGraw-Hill Book Company, 1979.

Moser, Harold. The Papers of Andrew Jackson: 1814-1815. Knoxville: The University of Tennessee Press, 1980.

Onuf, Peter S. Jeffersonian Legacies. University Press of Virginia, 1993.

Peterson, Merrill. Thomas Jefferson: Writings. New York: Literary Classics of the United States, Inc., 1984.

Peterson, Merrill. James Madison: A Biography of His Own Words. New York: Harper & Row Publishers, Inc., 1974.

Powell, Lawrence N. Northern Planters During the Civil War and Reconstruction. Fordham University Press, 1998.

Pryor, Elizabeth B. Reading the Man: A Portrait of Robert E. Lee Through His Private Letters. New York: Penguin Books, 2008.

Randall, Willard S. George Washington: A Life. New York: Henry Holt and Company, 1997.

Rees, James. George Washington's Leadership Lessons. Hoboken, NJ: John Wiley & Sons, Inc., 2007.

Remini, Robert V. The Life of Andrew Jackson. New York: Harper & Row, Publishers, 1988.

Rutland, Robert A. James Madison: The Founding Father. New York: MacMillan Publishing Company, 1987.

Scarborough, William K. Masters of the Big House: Elite Slaveholders of the Mid-Nineteenth-Century South. LSU Press, 2006.

Schneider, Dorothy. Slavery in America: An Eyewitness History. New York: Checkmark Books, 2007.

Smith, Margaret Bayard. The First Forty Years of Washington Society, Scribner, 1906.

Stone, Ormond & W.T. Myers. Alumni Bulletin of the University of Virginia, Third Series, Vol. V, Charlottesville, 1912.

Wiencek, Henry. An Imperfect God: George Washington, His Slaves, and the Creation of America. New York: Farrar, Strauss and Giroux, 2003.

Yarbrough, Jean. (Jefferson, Thomas.) The Essential Jefferson. Indianapolis: Hackett Publishing Company, Inc., 2006.

Periodicals

Maryland Gazette

National Anti-Slavery Standard: (April 14, 1866 - fair-use.org)

New York Daily Tribune: (Letter from a Citizen, June 24, 1859.)

New York Times

Notes

---

[1] Ferling, 68. Randall, 207.

[2] Marrin, 71.

[3] Maryland Gazette (Annapolis), 8/20/1761, George Washington. Randall, 207-08.

[4] Mountvernon.org

[5] Wiencek, 95.

[6] Ferling, 478. Hirschfeld, 37.

[7] Randall, 259.

[8] The Papers of George Washington: The Confederation Series, Volume 4, Letter to Robert Morris, Apr. 12, 1786. Lodge, 157. Rees, 7. Wiencek, 99.

[9] Dudley, 70.

[10] Farmbook, 7. Onuf, 156. McLaughlin, 110.

[11] McLaughlin, 113.

[12] Betts, 442. McLaughlin, 112. Onuf, 158.

[13] McLaughlin, 113.

[14] McLaughlin, 96. Foley, 814. Letter to Edward Coles.

[15] McLaughlin, 144.

[16] Foley, 812, 813. Notes on Virginia. Schneider, 88. Jefferson, 22. Draft of the Declaration of Independence.

[17] Peterson, "Writings" 44. Foley, 816. Randall, 302. Bernstein, 62.

[18] Peterson, "Writings" 264, 1485. Yarbrough, 257. Foley, 623. Jefferson, 149.

[19] McLaughlin, 97, 98. Betts, 46.

[20] Jefferson, 175. Peterson, "Writings" 288.

[21] Foley, 621. McLaughlin, 96. Letter to Edward Coles.

[22] Foley, 811. Schneider, 265. Peterson, 288, 1433. Jefferson, 175. Letter to M. De Meunier.

[23] Moore, 391. Stone, 50.

[24] Smith, 81. Moore, 228.

[25] Ketcham, 428. Peterson, "A Biography" 214-16.

[26] Hillard, 347. Peterson, "A Biography" 368.

[27] Jennings, 7-8.

[28] Jennings, 20-21.

[29] Moore, 125. Rutland, 92.

[30] Jennings, 6, 16-17.

[31] Elliott, 458. Debates on the Adoption of the Federal Constitution, Reported by James Madison.
[32] Peterson, "A Biography" 373.
[33] Peterson, "A Biography" 377.
[34] Bassett, 302. Meacham, 291. Remini, 279.
[35] Meacham, 93, 95. Rogin, 147.
[36] Schneider, 271.
[37] Jackson Papers, Aug. 21, 1814.
[38] James, "Life" 348. Meacham, 302-03. Remini, 52. Nashville's Tennessee Gazette, Sept. 26, 1804.
[39] Feller, 333. James, 544.
[40] Moser, 162.
[41] Moser, 194.
[42] James, 758, 785.
[43] Scarborough, 14, 23. Brazy, 13.
[44] Scarborough, 185.
[45] Brazy, 30.
[46] Brazy, 53.
[47] Scarborough, 207. Brazy, 54.
[48] Brazy, 58.
[49] Brazy, 62.
[50] Brazy, 65-66.
[51] Gower, 142. Scarborough, 222, 236. Brazy, 111.
[52] Gower, 74, 142.
[53] Brazy, 118.
[54] Brazy, 128.
[55] Brazy, 129.
[56] Powell, 45. Gower, 143. New York Times, December 21, 1860.
[57] Davis, V., 12.
[58] Davis, V., 178. Davis, W., 81, 188-89.
[59] Allen, 91, 168. Hattaway, 6, 12.
[60] Allen, 115.
[61] Cooper, 69, 114. Hattaway, 9, 12.
[62] Crist, 12. New York Times, Jan. 11, 1863 [from Richmond Enquirer, Jan. 7, 1863].
[63] Crist, 135, 206, 207, 217.
[64] George Johnson interview, Sept. 1941.
[65] Pryor, 125, 126.

[66] National Anti-Slavery Standard, Apr. 14, 1866. Pryor, 260. Blassingame, 467.
[67] New York Daily Tribune, June 24, 1859.
[68] Cairnes, 70, 105. Pryor, 134.
[69] Pryor, 123-124. Letter to Mr. A. E. L. Keese from R. E. Lee on Apr. 24, 1858.
[70] Pryor, 266.
[71] Pryor, 128, 129, 263.
[72] Long, 83. Pryor, 144, 268, 269.
[73] Dowdey, 107, 350, 378, 379.
[74] Lee, 89, 231.
[75] Schneider, 326. Washington D.C. M.C.